1975

PASSIONATE INTELLIGENCE

Sam Johnson

PASSIONATE INTELLIGENCE

Imagination and Reason in the Work of Samuel Johnson

by Arieh Sachs

The Johns Hopkins Press, Baltimore

For Celia and Mendes

CONTENTS

ACKNOWLEDGEMENTS

I am deeply indebted to George Boas, Georges Poulet, Don Cameron Allen, Earl R. Wasserman and J. Hillis Miller, the men whose admirable teaching first drew me to literary study. Enid Welsford, Adam Mendilow, Daniel Fineman and Zwi Werblowsky were sources of both good advice and encouragement at a later stage, when I was writing the essay on Johnson from which this book has grown. Dorothea Krook graciously provided me with her 1825 edition of Johnson's Works.

The Modern Humanities Research Association of Great Britain and the Editors of the *Modern Language Review*, *Studies in English Literature 1500–1900*, *Studies in Philology*, *English Studies* and the *Scripta Hierosolymitana Series* have kindly tolerated publication, in revised form, of material which had appeared earlier in various articles.

I also wish to record the unfailing courtesy of the Johns Hopkins editors J. G. Goellner, Barbara Parmelee and Anne C. Ambrose.

INTRODUCTION

*J*ohnson's observations on many subjects have in common the basic notion of a polarity of faculties: Reason and Imagination. This is the polarity that equally underlies the religious, the moral, the political, the aesthetic, and the psychological phases of his thought. In the *Dictionary*, Imagination is defined as (among other things) "the power of forming *ideal* pictures" or "the power of presenting things *absent*," and these are in fact the senses in which Johnson most frequently uses the term. But a full understanding of the underpinning of his thought involves an extended meaning. The faculty of Imagination as opposed to that of Reason ultimately denotes a power in man which increases the inherent incompatibility between his bodily and his mental modes of being, or, interchangeably, between that in man which is temporal and that which is extratemporal. It is Imagination that projects itself beyond presentness and actuality, fixes upon objects that are distant in time or space, and imbues them with value. Imagination is the great overreacher. All human "uneasiness" about earthly affairs, whether the anxious forward-projection of hope and fear or the equally tense backward-projection of obsessive memory, is produced by Imagination. Imagination transforms the unspecified into the specific, directs desire and aversion toward particular earthly goals, and is behind man's futile pursuit of absolute "happiness" within time. It is the power that is forever trying to halt time by means of its metamorphosing action upon temporal reality. In imaginative "memory," it projects itself backwards in time, creating delusive obsessions with either the glamor or the horror of past experience, forming imaginary Golden Ages, personal states of absolute bliss, or, conversely, total guilt. In its extreme form it becomes overt madness, for its culmination is a complete loss of contact with reality.

Imagination not only moves forwards and backwards in time but, so to speak, upwards as well, "speculating" on questions of metaphysical import, reducing to rigid formulae what is outside the sphere of limited human knowledge. Not only the idea of a Cosmic Hierarchy, but all "meteors of philosophy" [1] are produced by this idealizing, delusive tendency: "the Cartesian, who denies that his horse feels the spur . . . the disciple of Malebranche, who maintains that the man was not hurt by the bullet . . . the follower of Berkeley, who while he sits writing at his table, declares that he has neither table, paper nor fingers" [2] are victims of the same fallacy. The Skeptic and the Stoic are in different ways its prey. It is Imagination that denies the primacy of experience and claims for itself the infallibility of godlike views, uncommitted and totally objective; views that in reality represent human subjectivity. Stoic detachment, supposedly rational, is seen by Johnson (and by many Christian thinkers before him) as springing from a loss of touch with what it means to be human. The same is true of the kind of scientism that is not oriented toward real use (not only in the utilitarian but in the older and wider sense of the *utile*) and of primitivism, with its idealization and glorification of exotic simplicity. All such views are condemned as "dangerous" to both religion and morality. In forming *ideal* pictures, Imagination is the great simplifier, for it springs from the human need for something absolute, immutable, and uncomplicated. Reason also functions in terms of this need, but Reason, through experience, learns to concentrate upon true absolutes—the ultimate truths of religion— where Imagination treats the relative and contingent as if they were absolutes.

On the religious level, Imagination manifests itself as pride and false security. It makes man treat his mortal life as if it were never to end. The custom of quotidianism, generated by Imagination, is the mark of man's lapsed state. On the moral level, Imagination appears as quixotism, obsessiveness, specialization, the "Choice of Life." On the political level it is what underlies fanaticism, utopianism, and the revolutionary impatience with those shortcomings in society that are necessary and inherent because they are produced by unchanging human creatureliness. Imagination sets

[1] *Rambler* No. 181, *Works*, III, 345.
[2] *Idler* No. 10, *Works*, IV, 179.

up Heavenly Cities on earth. In doing so it becomes the root of war, discord, and faction. On the aesthetic level it is the mainspring of freakish romances, of "ideal" literature (the pastoral, for example), and of partial depictions of detail at the expense of the extensive (yet humanly committed and observant) view of the whole.[3]

Reason is the diametrical opposite of Imagination. It is the faculty in man which keeps him in contact with his true state. It is that which diminishes the incompatibility between the bodily (or temporal) and the mental (or supratemporal) by providing man with "general" estimates both of his limitations and of his capacities. In religion, Reason is the secret of spiritual regeneration, of the "Choice of Eternity," the religious hope and fear that completely negate earthly, imaginative desire and aversion; for the focal point of religious hope and fear is man's true destiny as apprehended by Reason. In his Prayers, Johnson asks to be "animated with *reasonable hope.*" [4] The religious fear of death and of punishment hereafter is no less rational: "If he who considers himself as suspended over the abyss of eternal perdition only by the thread of life, which must soon part by its own weakness, and which the wing of every minute may divide, can cast his eyes round him without shuddering with horror . . . he is not yet awakened" [5] to truly *reasonable* fear.

In morals Reason is the mainspring of right action, synonymous with virtue, for virtue is the exercise of reason. In politics, Reason is at the core of all enlightened yet realistic and tradition-respecting policy. In aesthetics it is the source of the delight and instruction which are the necessary ingredients of real poetic worth. Reason manifests itself in art through the true portrayal of that which is constant and abiding in Nature and in Life, that which transcends time.

Such a summary is admittedly crude. All the terms I have been using—whether "narrow," "general," "nature," "obsession," "hope and fear," "pride," and even "time"—appear here in a special sense, and the reader is referred to the following chapters for my attempt to clarify such notions in terms of Christian-Humanist tradition, of

[3] Imagination and fancy for Johnson are interchangeable terms. But Johnson does sometimes use these terms in his criticism to designate something different from what I have been discussing, i.e., poetic *inventiveness.*

[4] *Diaries,* p. 74.

[5] *Rambler* No. 110, *Works,* III, 23.

Johnson's life, and of that which is recurrent in his writings and conversation. I do not think, for example, that Johnson's idea of Imagination can be understood apart from his basic ideas on the "vacuity of life," apart from his personal struggle with "indolence" and the "chain of sin," or apart from the diabolical associations the word had acquired throughout the centuries of faith. "His laboring brain/Begets a world of *idle fantasies*," says Mephistophilis of Faustus in Marlowe's play (V. ii. 14–5). Underlying this is a conception of Imagination that is radically closer to Johnson's than anything to be found in post-Augustan literature. One of my points in this book is that Johnson usually employs the term Imagination in a sense lost to romantic and modern usage, but very much alive in medieval and Renaissance English literature. Much Augustan literature is best studied as a product of the late Renaissance, the culmination of many centuries of basically homogeneous civilization. The medieval element in Johnson's thought is, as I try to show, strong, and in more than one way. The conventional view of him as a representative of the English "Common Sense School" certainly does not do him justice.

What is perhaps important to stress in this attempt at an introduction is the fact that Johnson always satirizes the human ideal of a *purely* rational state, completely released from the tensions which vacuity, lapsedness, passion, and imaginative projection of one kind or another produce. His ideal is rather the regulation and control of imaginative impulse through rational awareness. Again, this is completely traditional, as I hope my quotations from the *Essay on Man*, *Gulliver's Travels*, and many earlier works will demonstrate. Human virtue, merit, enduring achievement, and worth are connected in Johnson's thought with religious redemption, as their opposites are connected with sin; but he always portrays the attainable goal of man in terms of a balance of Reason and Imagination, or rather in terms of a true ordering and control of impulse by lucidity. Imagination, which superficially appears to be man's "lower" faculty, is really on a par with Reason, the "higher" faculty, in that it is a given constituent of human nature and in that all attempts to disregard this fact are in themselves manifestations of man's imaginative folly. The real goal for man is the exercise of the kind of rational imagination and passionate intelligence which lead to virtuous action, whereas the vain attempt to become a "superior being" or to see humanity from an

xiv

angelically rational point of view inevitably ends in something that is below the potential dignity of man. Most frequently it ends in cruelty, stupidity, and degradation. True human dignity is the exercise of both human tendencies, the rational and the imaginative, through the submission of impulse and desire to the control of reason and to a courageous confrontation of the painful facts of human futility and guilt.

Rasselas, perhaps the fullest statement of Johnson's ideas on many subjects, is, I shall try to show, a deeply Christian book. A large proportion of the *Ramblers*, *Idlers*, and *Adventurers* are really no less religious in intent than the Sermons or the Prayers and Meditations. Johnson's moral teaching is an extension of his religious belief, just as his aesthetic doctrine is an extension of his morality. None of his work can be understood apart from his faith, for "his piety [was] the ruling principle of all his conduct."[6] One of my main aims in this book is thus to show in what sense his views on highly diverse subjects spring from the primacy of his orthodox Christianity.

But the primacy of religion in his work should not obscure his extreme relevance to an unbelieving age. Johnson should be read in the same spirit as one reads Pascal. He is the greatest moralist in English—not in the sense that he had a new system of ethics to offer, but in the sense that he was the most original rethinker of a great cultural heritage. Among English moralists, it was he who most richly and pithily summed up the abiding meaning (and meaninglessness) of human existence. There is nothing dead about his works. His religious pessimism may serve as an antidote— whether we share his theism or not—for the kind of pettiness, complacency, and ridiculous self-satisfaction that seem to be the companions of abundance and technological advance. His morality is ever-relevant: if ever there was a man who exemplified in both his life and his work the difficult, Jobian, unsentimental meaning of human goodness, it was Johnson. His distrust of all perfectionism in politics surely has meaning in a century that has committed its worst crimes in the name of high-flown abstractions and fanatical idealisms. His rigorous aesthetics, the distrust of "vain fancy" in many kinds of literature, and the insistence that only what can endure has merit are entirely to the point in a society that seems increasingly to regard as "art" what is mere entertainment, ephemeral shock-effect, or sheer escapism.

[6] *Life*, IV, 429.

PASSIONATE INTELLIGENCE

CHAPTER ONE: THE VACUITY OF LIFE

*T*hat human life is in a special sense *"vacuous"* is a recurrent idea in Johnson and may be seen as the starting point of his thought on many subjects. To understand its meaning is to understand the way in which his observations on a great variety of topics are guided by the implicit polarities of eternity and time, reason and imagination, expectation and existence, speculation and fact.

Johnson's basic metaphor for human experience is the empty receptacle which cannot tolerate its own emptiness. The mind has an insatiated craving to be "filled" by ever-new "objects of attention" which it discards as soon as they have become familiar. It exists in time, and time, to satisfy it, must do what it cannot do, supply it with eternal "novelty." "The old peripatetick principle that *Nature abhors a vacuum* may be properly applied to the mind," [1] but the vacuous mind, preying hungrily on experience, can never satisfy its gnawing need to be filled. The essential dichotomy in Johnson's concept of the mental vacuum is between this inherent need of the mind to be filled with "objects of attention" and the elusive nature of the objects offered it by temporal experience. The mind, surpassing its immediate experience, ultimately is beyond all possible earthly experience; for it operates on reality through acts of imagination that prevent it from staying with anything that is close at hand. The soul and the will are infinite, the objectifications of will in the temporal flow of life finite, and that is why life is inherently unsatisfactory—not merely because of some contingent misery or special misfortune.

The initial state of the human mind is a kind of metaphysical ennui into which fresh ideas must be "poured" and "curiosity kept in a perpetual motion" [2] if it is not to stagnate in subjectivity. "Vacancy" implies the total blankness and neutrality of

[1] *Rambler* No. 85, *Works*, II, 402.
[2] *Rambler* No. 89, *Works*, II, 419.

3

consciousness as it is in itself, apart from its experience. All energy and all activity are caused by man's essential need to escape this vacuity, by his need "*to fill the vacancies of attention*, and lessen the tediousness of time."[3] For example, "if you shut up any Man and Woman for six Months together, so as to make them derive all their Pleasures from each other, they would inevitably fall in Love; but if at the end of that Term you would throw each of them into Assemblies, and let them change Partners at Pleasure, they would soon forget their mutual *Attachment; which nothing but the necessity of some Connection, & the vacuity of life had caused.*"[4]

This central theme of Johnson's thought went quite unnoticed by Boswell, and it was left to the sophisticated Mrs. Thrale to note that "Johnson who thinks *the vacuity of Life* the source of ye passions, says it is certainly so both with regard to Love and Friendship,"[5] and to recount how "somebody would say—Such a Lady never touches a Card—how then does She get rid of *her Time* says Johnson, does she drink Drams? Such a Person never suffers Gentlemen to buzz in his Daughter's Ears: who is to buzz in her Ears then?—the Footman!"[6] And Mrs. Thrale even went so far as to recognize the relation of such lighthearted observations to Johnson's central theme and obsessing image. "The vacuity of Life," she suggests,

had at some early period of his life perhaps so struck upon the Mind of Mr. Johnson, that it became by repeated impressions his favourite hypothesis, & the general Tenor of his reasonings commonly ended in that: The Things therefore which other philosophers attribute to various and contradictory Causes appeared to him uniform enough; all was done to fill up the time upon his Principle. One Man for example was profligate, followed the Girls or the Gaming Table,—why Life *must* be filled up Madam, & the man was capable of nothing less Sensual. Another was active in the management of his Estate & delighted in domestic Economy: Why a Man *must do something*, & what so easy to a narrow Mind as hoarding halfpence till they turn into Silver?[7]

I think that Mrs. Thrale is especially acute in speaking of vacuity not only as Johnson's "favourite hypothesis" but also as

---

[3] *Rasselas*, chap. i, p. 39.
[4] *Thraliana*, I. 198.
[5] *Ibid.*, p. 254.
[6] *Ibid.*, p. 193. Cf., p. 355: "Johnson says Women who will not work and cannot play at Cards must drink Drams of necessity."
[7] *Ibid*, p. 179.

"the general tenor of his reasonings." [8] Where the vacuity of life is not the explicit theme of his writings or conversation, it is present as the underlying assumption and constantly shows up in the imagery. All human activity is seen as a futile attempt to fill an aching inner void, an incessant and hopeless search for "novelty" and "diversity" with which to feed the hunger of the mind. The imagery of emptiness and filling-up appears in such phrases as "every diversity of nature pours ideas in upon the soul," [9] and explicit statements of the theme in Johnson's moral writings are quite numerous:

All our gratifications are volatile, vagrant, and easily dissipated. The fragrance of the jessamine bower is lost after the enjoyment of a few moments, and the Indian wanders among his native spices without any sense of their exhalations. It is, indeed, not necessary to shew by many instances what all mankind confess, by *an incessant call for variety, and restless pursuit of enjoyments, which they value only because unpossessed.* . . . The most important events, when they become familiar, are no longer considered with wonder and solicitude, and that which at first *filled up our whole attention, and left no place for any thought,* is soon thrust aside into some remote repository of the mind, and lies among other lumber of the memory, overlooked and neglected.[10]

In the *Dictionary* a large proportion of the meanings Johnson distinguishes in the words "vacancy" and "vacuity" refers to this mental emptiness.[11] In Boswell we find Johnson struck by "Madame [de] Sévigné, who, though she had many enjoyments, felt with

---

[8] Among Johnson's modern commentators, W. J. Bate, in his illuminating study *The Achievement of Samuel Johnson* (New York, 1955), and Robert Voitle in *Samuel Johnson The Moralist* (Cambridge, Mass, 1961), pay some attention to Johnson's "favourite hypothesis." The present study owes much to their analyses.

[9] *Idler* No. 44, *Works*, IV, 279.

[10] *Rambler* No. 78, *Works*, II, 366, 367.

[11] Many of the passages he quotes to illustrate these meanings bear out the personal set of connotations he attaches to the word. E.g.,

"VACANCY 5. Listlessness; emptiness of thought. 'When alone, or in company, they sit still without doing anything, I like it worse; for all dispositions to idleness or *vacancy*, even before they are habits are dangerous.' *Wotton*

VACANT 2. Free; unencumbered; uncrowded. 'Religion is the interest of all; but philosophy of those only that are at leisure, and *vacant* from the affairs of the world.' *More's Divine Dialogues.* 'A very little part of life is so vacant from uneasiness as to leave us free to the attraction of some remoter good.' *Locke* 4. Being at leisure; disengaged. '. . . The memory relieves the mind in her *vacant* moments, and prevents any chasms of thought by ideas of what is past.' *Addison* 5. Thoughtless; empty of thought; not busy. 'The wretched slave/Who, with body filled and *vacant* mind,/Gets him to rest, crammed with distressful bread.' *Shakes.* 'Some vain amusement of a vacant soul.' *Irene*"

5

delicate sensibility the prevalence of misery, and complains of the task of existence having been imposed upon her without her consent." [12] His comment is: "That *man is never happy for the present* is so true, that all his relief from unhappiness is only forgetting himself for a little while. Life is a *progress from want to want, not from enjoyment to enjoyment.*" [13] As for *Rasselas*, its central theme is, of course, precisely that hope is futile not because particular hopes end in disappointment, though this is the empirically observable outcome of the human condition, but because it is in the nature of earthly hope, which is the supreme manifestation of initial vacuity and craving, to be frustrated by reality in the end.[14]

Hope is the action of the mind transcending itself, but the objects of hope are temporal, so that they necessarily remain behind. The difference between the various objects hope fixes on is superficial. The mind may choose wealth, power, sensual pleasure, even knowledge, as the proper object of its desire, but in the end the desire itself and the fact that it is infinite will make all those finite ends equally "insufficient." The elusive present can never, by definition, be really satisfactory; the mind, continuing its temporal movement beyond present fulfillments, inevitably imagines something else that is more desirable, or even more of what it already has but which it values precisely because it is not yet fully possessed. The only real experience available to the vacuous mind, which incessantly craves new "presentness," is that which disappears into the past as soon as it has emerged from the future. Consequently, it throws itself back into the past, to memories that are largely of its own invention, by an act of imagination that tries absurdly to overcome the frustration of real temporal experience in an illusion of past glamor; or, by a similar act of imagination that tries absurdly to transcend time, it reaches into the future and fixes on objects of hope—Johnson often calls it "expectation"—which it makes in the image of its need. Obviously, these objects of hope can never, in the strict sense of the word, materialize.

[12] *Life*, III, 53. Hill quotes Madame de Sévigné, writing her daughter (March 16, 1672): "Je me trouve dans un engagement qui m'embarasse: je suis embarquée dans la vie sans mon consentement . . . si on m'avait demandé mon avis j'aurais bien aimé à mourir entre les bras de ma nourrice." (*ibid*, n.2.).

[13] *Life*, III, 53.

[14] For other instances of the "vacuity of life" see, e.g., *Thraliana*, pp. 179–80, 193–199, 254, 355. Among the early writings, *Ramblers* No. 2 and No. 8 stand out as full statements of the theme.

"We represent to ourselves the pleasures of some future possession, and suffer our thoughts to dwell attentively upon it, till it has wholly engrossed the imagination," [15] but the mind will be as vacuous and "hungry" when the object of its hope becomes present. "The *deceitfulness of hope*"[16] and "*the fallacies by which mortals are deluded*" [17] thus form another of Johnson's great themes: hope is "a Bubble which by a gentle Breath may be blown to a large Size, but a rough Blast bursts it at once." [18] In the *Adventurer*, he writes that "it is easy for the imagination, *operating on things not yet existing*, to please itself with scenes of *unmingled felicity*," [19] and in the *Idler*: "fancy dances after meteors of happiness kindled by itself." [20] "He that has pictured a prospect *upon his fancy*, will receive little pleasure from *his eyes*." [21]

This unbridgeable gap between the image created by the mind as it throws itself into the future, and the reality of that future when once it has emerged into the present, is the true reason why one can speak of "the insufficiency of wealth, honours, and power to real happiness" [22]—which is the theme of Johnson's greatest poem, *The Vanity of Human Wishes*. Like all of Johnson's recurrent themes, his analysis of hope is generalized from his own experience and is also applied back to it. In a letter to Baretti, for example, he wrote:

Last winter I went down to my native town, where I *found the streets narrower and shorter than I thought I had left them*, inhabited by a new race of people, to whom I was very little known. My play-fellows were grown old, and forced me to suspect that I was no longer young. My only remaining friend had changed his principles and was become the tool of the predominant faction. My daughter-in-law, from whom I had expected most and whom I met with sincere benevolence, has lost the beauty and gaiety of youth, without having gained much of the wisdom of age. . . . Moral sentences appear ostentatious and tumid, when they have no greater occasion than the journey of a wit to his own town: yet such pleasures and pains make up the general mass of life; and as nothing is little to him that feels it with great sensibility,[23] a mind able to see things in their real state is disposed by very

[15] *Rambler* No. 17, *Works*, II, 83.
[16] *Idler* No. 59, *Works*, IV, 323.
[17] *Rambler* No. 54, *Works*, II, 259.
[18] *Thraliana*, I, 202.
[19] *Adventurer* No. 108, *Works*, IV, 101.
[20] *Idler* No. 41, *Works*, IV, 271.
[21] *Idler* No. 58, *Works*, IV, 322.
[22] *Rambler* No. 54, *Works*, II, 259.
[23] Cf., above, Johnson's comment on Mme. de Sévigné's "delicate sensibility [to] the prevalence of misery." What such sensibility comes to for Johnson is simply an acute sense of fact.

common incidents to very serious contemplations. Let us trust the time will come, when *the present moment shall be no longer irksome;* when we *shall not borrow all our happiness from hope, which at last is to end in disappointment.*[24]

His "sensibility" to examples of the futility of expectation, a futility which ultimately he saw as the very definition of human existence on earth, extended from life to literature (which was at its best for him when it justly portrayed "general nature," i.e., the human condition). His close readings of poetry became especially pointed, acute, and sensitive when the theme was the futility of hope. On "Pope's melancholy remark, 'Man never *is*, but always *to be* blest,' " [25] he "enlarged," reports Boswell, with the comment "that the *present* was never a happy state to any human being; but that, as every part of life, of which we are conscious, was at some point of time a period yet to come, in which felicity was expected, there was some happiness produced by hope." [26] Of the lines,

> *Thou hast nor youth, nor age,*
> *But as it were an after-dinner's sleep,*
> *Dreaming on both,*[27]

he says, "This is exquisitely imagined. When we are young *we busy ourselves in forming schemes for succeeding time, and miss the gratifications that are before us;* when we are old we *amuse the langour of age with the recollection of youthful pleasures or performances;* so that our life, *of which no part is filled with the business of the present time,* resembles our dreams after dinner." [28] Johnson's qualified approbation of Cowley's "Against Hope,"

> *Hope, whose weak Being ruin'd is,*
> *Alike if it succeed, and if it miss;*
> *Whom Good and Ill does equally confound,*
> *And both the Horns of Fates Dilemma wound,*

which follows in the *Life of Cowley* much unqualified disapproval of other metaphysical poems, may also be traced to his special concern with the topic and to his agreement with Cowley's sentiments; although one can only guess why Johnson justifies his approval by saying that hope is a subject upon

[24] 20 July 1762, in *Letters*, I, 139–40.
[25] Alexander Pope, *Essay on Man*, Epistle I, l. 96.
[26] *Life*, II, 351.
[27] *Measure for Measure*, III. i.
[28] *On Shakespeare*, p. 78.

which "scholastick speculation can be properly admitted." [29] But the fallacy of hope always represents for Johnson the triumph of Imagination over Reason, due to the mind's vacuous and futile obsessions.

Ultimately, Imagination, which is the mind's obsessive tendency to limit itself to some particular earthly goal or object as a result of its inherent incompatibility with temporal experience, is associated with madness. Earthly hope, is the product of Imagination, that part in man which is out of touch with reality, and of the incessant craving of the mind to be filled with objects "pleasing to itself"— objects which reality does not and cannot supply. But hope is not something one can take or leave alone; it is woven into the fabric of life itself, the inevitable mark of human existence in time. As Johnson puts it in his chapter on "the prevalence of imagination" in *Rasselas*, life itself implies universal madness: "Perhaps, if we speak with rigorous exactness, no human mind is in its right state. There is no man whose imagination does not, sometimes, predominate over his reason. . . . No man will be found, in whose mind airy notions do not, sometimes, tyrannize, and force him *to hope or fear beyond the limits of probability*. All power of fancy over reason is a degree of insanity." [30]

Man's need for "diversion" and "novelty" thus entails perpetual illusion. The unsatisfactoriness of the present leads him to "expatiate in boundless futurity" and "cull, from all imaginable conditions, that which, for the present moment, he should most desire." [31] This becomes a habit, until the mind automatically "feasts on the luscious falsehood whenever she is offended with the bitterness of truth" [32] and then literal madness has set in. The syllogism is simple: hope, which is the necessary concomitant of existence, is the observable outcome of the "prevalence of imagination"; imagination prevailing over the rational recognition of the true state of affairs makes for madness; it follows that existence itself, which forces us to "regale our mind with airy gratifications," [33] has absurdity and madness at its core.

[29] *Life of Cowley, Works,* VI, 37.
[30] *Rasselas,* chap. xliv, pp. 139–140.
[31] *Ibid.*
[32] *Ibid.*
[33] *Rambler* No. 89, *Works,* II, 417.

The insufficiency of the world to the spirit of man is a commonplace. In the third century B.C., the mysterious Preacher of *Ecclesiastes* was maintaining that "the eye is not satisfied with seeing, nor the ear filled hearing" (1:8), that "he loveth silver shall not be satisfied with silver, nor he that loveth abundance with increase" (5:10), and that in human experience "that which is wanting cannot be numbered" (1:15). In the seventeenth century Donne was meditating "upon this *great world, Man,* so far, as to consider the immensitie of the creatures this world produces; our *creatures* are our *thoughts,* creatures that are borne *Gyants;* that reach from *East* to *West,* from Earth to *Heaven,* that do not only bestride all the *Sea,* and *Land,* but span the Sun and Firmament at once. . . . My thoughts reach all, comprehend all. Inexplicable mistery: I their creator am in a close prison." [34] In the nineteenth century, Walter Bagehot dryly remarked that "taken as a whole, the universe is absurd. There seems an unalterable contradiction between the human mind and its employments." [35]

The Johnsonian axiom that the human condition is defined by the boredom which results from the incompatibility between the soul's infinite desires and the finite quality of the experience available to it in the elusive temporality of life, that the futility of temporal existence is demonstrated by the fact that "no man can at pleasure obtund or invigorate his senses, prolong the agency of any impulse, or continue the presence of any image traced upon the eye, or any sound infused upon the ear," [36] would appear therefore to be a mere reaffirmation of an oft-repeated truth. But the central assumptions of Johnson's thought, and in particular the idea that the secret of earthly value lies in the mind's obsessions and that these obsessions are generated by the mind's initial "vacuity," gain added depth and force when viewed in terms of Johnson's particular being, in terms, that is, of his biography. "Nothing is more common than to call our own condition, the condition of life," [37] we are told in *Rasselas,* and surely nowhere is the truth of this statement more apparent than in the case of Johnson himself. The natural movement of his mental processes was to follow upon and generalize from highly personal

[34] John Donne *Devotions Upon Emergent Occasions,* ed. J. Sparrow (Cambridge, 1923) pp. 13–16 (IV, Meditation).
[35] *Literary Studies* (4th ed.; London, 1891), I, 36.
[36] *Rambler* No. 78, *Works,* II, 367.
[37] *Rasselas,* chap. xlv, p. 144.

experience, so that all his ideas about the general human situation are in an important sense an extension of private sensibility.

Neoclassical though his attitude to language was, his use of words is no less charged with connotations than that of the most romantic or symbolistic of poets, and it is with due regard to this charged quality of his language that his prose should be read. Phrases like "to fix the attention," "to dwell attentively" upon something, to let something "get possession of your thoughts," "prevail over the mind" or "preoccupy the soul," all key phrases in both Johnson's writings and conversation, reveal their full meaning only when we relate them to the context of his particular—essentially private—mode of experience; when we take into account personal connotation as well as public denotation. The *Times Literary Supplement* reviewer of the Yale edition of Johnson's diaries failed to realize this when he made the conventional separation between the anguished Johnson "shut in his den" and "that other Johnson who really matters—Johnson the public figure and talker." [38] There was, in fact, only one Johnson. His public statements are charged with a meaning that is more directly expressed in what he wrote when he confronted himself in solitude and are generalized from that solitary experience. The "public figure" is a sentimentalized fiction unless seen as that very same man.

Johnson's concept of the "vacuity of life" was abstracted from an experience of mental blankness and stagnation that had nothing general or formal about it. *Au fond*, "vacuity of life" simply means a severe form of personal boredom. In the same way Imagination was derived from his conviction that he had the seed of madness within him. In *Rasselas* madness is a recurrent theme, and Johnson's own mind, like that of the mad hermit and the mad Astronomer he portrayed in his moral tale, had firsthand knowledge of that peculiar staleness and paralysis of will, that accidie which drives the mind to turn upon itself for imaginative wish fulfillments. Like his brain children, Johnson's own dread and terror were intensified by a powerful consciousness of sin bordering on criminal despair. His was a "disease of the imagination . . . which is complicated with the dread of guilt," in which "fancy and conscience . . . act interchangeably" [39] and which, in religious terms, meant a constant

[38] *Times Literary Supplement* (London), March 6, 1959, pp. 121–2.
[39] *Rasselas*, chap. xlvi, p. 149.

walking of the tightrope over an abyss of despair. Johnson tells us that the astronomer's mind was clouded by the gloom of solitude until its constant introspection and highly developed sense of guilt—for he was a man of superior intelligence and parts—became so unbearable that he was driven to seek refuge in the mad belief that he was God's Chosen and could regulate the weather at will. His inactivity and isolation from the world stimulated his imagination until finally his reason lost control.[40] In the same way the hermit, living a life of solitude, introspection, and lack of involvement in the real moral concerns of mankind, finally discovers that his mind has begun "to riot with scenes of folly," [41] to lose all contact with reality. Both the astronomer and the hermit are projections. They serve as a kind of self-diagnosis for a man who felt himself constantly at the point of madness and who could not help but indulge himself in that indolence and "immoderate sleep" which he at the same time felt to be morally a waste of precious time, psychologically a laying-open of the mind to melancholy, madness, and despair, and, religiously, to be his most grievous transgression against the will of God.

Johnson did not tire of confessing to his friends that "he always felt an inclination to do nothing," [42] that he was "an idle fellow all his life," [43] and that he allowed no excuse for it.[44] Both Hawkins and Murphy noted his guilt-ridden sloth,[45] and Boswell—who observed with obvious justice as far as the external facts were concerned that "it was strange to think that the most indolent man in Britain had written the most laborious work, THE ENGLISH DICTIONARY" [46]—nevertheless records, year after year, Johnson's melancholy insistence that he was "an idle fellow." [47] Johnson saw himself as suffering from a "frigid and narcotick infection," [48] a

[40] *Ibid.*, chap. xl *et seq.*, pp. 133–142.
[41] *Ibid.*, chap. xxi, p. 89.
[42] *Life*, I, 463.
[43] *Ibid.*, 465.
[44] *Ibid.*, IV, 9.
[45] For Arthur Murphy see *Life*, I, 268, n. 4 and 307, n. 2; for Sir John Hawkins, *Life*, III, 98, n. 1.
[46] *Life*, I. 463.
[47] In his boyhood—*Life*, I, 48, 50, 56; at College—*ibid.*, I, 70, n. 3; in 1760— *ibid.*, I, 353; in 1761—*ibid.*, I, 358; in 1763—*ibid.*, I, 398; in 1764—*ibid.*, I, 482; in 1767—*ibid.*, II, 44.
[48] *Rambler* No. 89, *Works*, II, 419.

chronic disease grounded in his physical constitution[49] and therefore
incurable. Guilt ridden, driven to despair of his salvation, we find
him in his diaries again and again recording renewed and desperate
resolutions to "shake off this sloth and to redeem the time misspent
in idleness and Sin," [50] and the theme is repeated throughout his
"public" pronouncements. His moral injunctions, his conversation,
his moral pamphlets and his letters to his friends turn upon the
slightest pretext to his obsession with the ways in which solitude
and idleness lead to despair and damnation. In a letter to Boswell,
praising the latter's decision to study law, he immediately points out
that by diligent application to his studies Boswell will "gain, at
least, what is no small advantage, security from those troublesome
and wearisome discontents, which are always obtruding themselves
upon *a mind vacant, unemployed, and undetermined.*" [51]

But the idea, derived from highly personal experience, is
characteristically generalized and extended, until it becomes part of
his definition of existence. In the eighty-fifth *Rambler* we are told
that "almost every occupation, however inconvenient or formidable,
is happier than the life of sloth. The necessity of action is . . .
demonstrable from the fabrick of the body." [52] That "vile
melancholy" which Johnson claimed he had "inherited from his
father" [53] never let go of him,[54] and he was convinced that he was
"mad, or at least not sober" most of his life.[55] He was extremely
interested in abnormal psychology and at one point even proposed
to write his own case history.[56] He was always on the lookout for
remedies against indolence[57] and developed an entire system of
complex moral thought out of his conviction that too much leisure
necessarily aggravated mental disorder[58] and that social activity was
its rational and religious cure. But the search for a cure never ended.
Mrs. Thrale was pointing to a mental state that persisted throughout
his life when she reported with her usual combination of insight and

[49] *Life*, I, 87, 203, 482.
[50] Easter, 1757, in *Diaries*, p. 63 *et passim.*
[51] *Life*, II, 21.
[52] *Rambler* No. 89, *Works*, II, 388.
[53] *Life*, I, 63, 343; IV, 300; IV, 2.
[54] *Ibid.*, I, 340, n. 1.
[55] *Ibid.*, 35, 65; V, 215.
[56] *Ibid.*, II, 45, n. 1.
[57] *Ibid.*, I, 190, 446; II, 440.
[58] See esp., *Rambler* No. 33, *Works*, II, 164.

glibness that "his over-anxious care to retain without blemish the perfect sanity of his mind, contributed much to disturb it. . . . He had studied medicine diligently in all its branches; but had given particular attention to the diseases of the imagination,[59] which he watched in himself with a solicitude destructive of his own peace, and intolerable to those he trusted."[60]

Johnson's greatness lies in his ability to transform his personal distress of melancholy, guilt, and indolence into impersonal observation. The experience of a desperately neurotic man was turned into a generalized scheme of morals and religion which could claim universal validity. Indolence became "vacuity," the obsessive "chain of sin" became "habit," neurotic fantasy became "imagination," and these notions were tied together in generalizations about mankind that on the whole are distinguished by their striking pertinence. Insisting that to achieve virtue and sanity (i.e., salvation) man must extricate himself from sterile introspection and—as Heraclitus put it—"follow what he has in common" with the rest of mankind, Johnson, in the highest sense, did precisely that. The starting point may have been the solitary

[59] One of Johnson's favorite medical authorities was George Cheyne, whose recommendations in matters like diet and tea-drinking he frequently referred to. See *Life*, I, 65; III, 26–27, 87, 152; IV, 3, 473; V, 154, 210. Johnson's notion that *the necessity of action is demonstrable from the fabric of the body* may well have originated in Cheyne's observation the "tho' Experience, which extremely confirms the Benefit of this Remedy [physical exercise] is the only solid Foundation to go upon, in the Cure of the Thing; yet the Reason of the Thing speaks so loudly, that it cannot but be hearken'd to by every reasonable Person. As *Diet* and *proper Medicine* in due time will certainly rectify the Juices, so Labour and Exercise will most infallibly strengthen the Solids, by promoting and continuing their constant Action and Motions." *The English Malady* (London, 1734), pp. 177–78. Further on Cheyne insists that those afflicted with nervous distempers should not only exercise their bodies but also provide constant diversion for their minds. Without "some amusement to employ themselves in . . . it seems absolutely impossible to keep the mind easy. . . . It is no matter what it is, provided it be but a *Hobby Horse*, and an Amusement, and stop the Current of Reflection and intense Thinking which Persons of weak nerves are aptest to run into" (pp. 181–82). The same recommendations may be found in earlier medical books. Lemnius, to relieve the "inconvenience which distempereth the mind" (L. L. Lemnius, *Touchstone of Complexions*, trans. T. Newton [London, 1565], leaf 145, *recto*), suggests diversions, games, and "Moderate myrth and banqueting" (leaf 154, *verso*). A medical treatise published in 1634 gives as a cause of melancholy, "studying without recreation or exercise of the body." I. M., *General Practice of Medicine* (London, 1634), sig. B2 and 3. The same idea appears in T. Bright, *Treatise of Melancholy* (London, 1586), pp. 300 *et seq.*, and, of course, in the conclusion of Robert Burton's *Anatomy of Melancholy*, which Johnson found so powerful (See *Life*, III, 415, and II, 440).

[60] Thrale-Piozzi, *Anecdotes, in J.M.*, I, 199–200.

Johnson suffering unspeakable frustration in his "den," but his very suffering was the ground from which grew the "public figure," as the *Times Literary Supplement* reviewer called him; the man who gave the world insights of the first order in criticism, morals, and religion.

From this point of view, Johnson's "madness" is responsible for his notion of what the life of virtue and piety consists in. Out of the connection between Vacuity and Imagination, between the "habitual drowsiness," "the state of neutrality or indifference," on the one hand, and "the luxury of fancy," "the art of regaling the mind with airy gratifications," the "invisible riot of the mind," the "secret prodigality of being," and the "sport of musing" in which the solitary dreamer of the eighty-ninth *Rambler* indulges, on the other, comes the notion of that *real* state of being which is its opposite, in which reason directs the mind to a life of contemplation, usefulness, and piety. Out of the sense of sin that gives rise to the damning notions of Vacuity and Imagination comes its opposite: the moralist's exhortation to virtue and to a rational "abstraction from the senses" in which the evil "habits" of life are overcome. The initial idea of vacuity-as-sin is complemented by an insistent emphasis on *activity*. Action becomes imbued with a deeply religious significance: action and objectivity both refer to a state of grace. When we think about life's span we must only consider maturity, not "the ignorance of infancy, or imbecility of age. We are, long before we are able to think, and we soon cease from the power of acting. The true period of human life may be reasonably estimated at forty years." [61] Such comments on the urgency of life, one of Johnson's recurrent themes, gain new meaning and coherence when we are familiar with the nature of Johnson's mental disorder and with his futile "resolutions" to act. Infancy and senility are immediately associated with subjectivity, imagination, paralysis of will and thought; and this paralysis with that personal indolence, sloth, and ennui Johnson firmly believed to be punishable by eternal damnation.

The insistence on the need to avoid self and subjectivity, to "teach one's desire to fix on external things," and, "in order to regain liberty, to find the means of flying from oneself," [62] equates the state of grace with activity on the one hand and with

[61] *Rasselas*, chap. iv, pp. 46–47.
[62] *Rambler* No. 89, *Works*, II, 418.

contemplative detachment from obsessive desires and hopes on the other. Johnson's belief in the indispensability of action to virtue and its function in liberating us from ourselves is paralleled and complemented by his repeated exhortation that we detach ourselves from any sort of total involvement in the present world of delusive hopes. To transcend the demands of the senses we must maintain a disengaged and contemplative state of mind, fixed not on the "Choice of Life" but on the "Choice of Eternity." The core of the argument lies in what both contemplation and virtuous action must break through, in the notion of *habit* which, like all else in his thought, is directly generalized from his own efforts to break "the chain of sin." Habit comes to mean the natural threat arising from existence in time. It is the normal state of man when he loses sight of his true situation because he is so totally *in* that situation. The vacuity of life leads to sensuality and subjectivity because it creates the habit of living according to the insatiate appetite of the senses. All virtue and all grace thus center on the loosening of the "chain of sin," the breaking of habitual fixations. In the seventh *Rambler* we are told that "we are in danger from whatever can *get possession of our thoughts*" and that "all that can excite in us either pleasure or pain has a tendency to obstruct our way to happiness." Existence itself involves "an hourly necessity of consulting the senses," so that mere sensual existence from moment to moment becomes habitual, and virtue, knowledge, and piety consequently need to be achieved through a conscious struggle with what existence-in-time itself dictates and is most deeply rooted in our nature.[63] In *Rasselas*, Imlac tells us that "pleasure" is in itself "harmless," but "may become mischievous, by *endearing to us* a state which we know to be transient and probatory, and *withdrawing our thoughts* from that, of which every hour brings us nearer to the beginning, and of which no length of time will bring us to the end." [64] "A constant residence amid noise and pleasure, *inevitably obliterates the impression of piety*," [65] so that there is a constant "necessity of *dispossessing the sensitive faculties* of the influence that they must naturally gain by this *preoccupation of the soul*." Only when we break the habit of being preoccupied with sensual hope and fear will "the motives to the

---

[63] *Works*, II, 30–4.
[64] *Rasselas* chap. xlvii, p. 152.
[65] *Rambler* No. 7, *Works*, II, 34.

life of holiness"—which in themselves are strong and convincing, since they are simply the dictates of reason—be able to "*gain our attention.*" [66]

This is where rationality and faith meet—in a state of contemplation and "repose" that is at once a disengagement from the mind's hungers, hopes, and fears and a total victory over the power of Imagination, the vehicle of those hungers and the supplier of mock fulfillments. This notion of a disengaged state of being, a notion directly derived from his personal need, guilt, and anguish, is the ideal Johnson sets up not only in his moral theories and as the goal of religious experience, but, in an important sense, as the point of departure for his literary criticism and aesthetic judgments as well. The famous critical dictum that "nothing can please long, but just representations of general nature" [67] is, after all, also the literary conclusion of his characteristic argument for a freedom from the falsifying tensions of self and imagination and from time itself; a freedom which can be provided only by "the stability of truth." "The irregular combinations of *fanciful invention* [i.e., imagination, the vacuity of life in search of objects] may *delight awhile,*" he writes in the *Preface to Shakespeare, "by that novelty of which the common satiety of life sends us all in quest;* but the pleasures of sudden wonder are soon exhausted, and the mind can only *repose on the stability of truth.*" The notion of truth as an ultimate criterion of value thus extends from morals and religion into art. It is one more instance of a religious rationalism that relates all human experience to the mind's fundamental struggle to be free of Imagination. Sanity, reason, virtue, and truth point at once both to religious salvation and to aesthetic worth: the "just portrayal of general nature" is the "Choice of Eternity" on the aesthetic level, a preference for the disclosures of pious Reason over the diabolical mirages of Imagination.

The *religious* state of mind in which "the stability of truth" is attained implies contact with one's actual state, objectively, in a full experience of mortality. For it is only the combination of "imagination" and "habit" that makes us forget death and enables us to live from moment to moment as if life were eternal. Imagination enables us to regard our finite ends as if they were infinite by stopping the flow of time for us. Habit confirms us in

---

[66] *Ibid.*, p. 33.
[67] *Preface to Shakespeare, Works,* III, 261.

our imaginative error, until it has become "radicated by time" and
is taken for granted—else all the striving of mankind after earthly
goals, which depends entirely on fundamental self-delusions and on
the habit of living from day to day, would have been impossible.
The rationality of religion manifests itself in its insistence on the
full experience of mortality, on the *objective* view of human life.
Reason itself discovers the truth of religion, because it is the initial
truth of the contradiction between the infinite desire of the mind
and the insufficiency and finitude of the temporal ends with which
the mind becomes obsessed. The full experience of mortality is
therefore the experience in which all Johnson's thought culminates,
for it opens up the *other* state of being—real being—as distinct from
the thoughtless vegetation of quotidian life. In *Rasselas*, this is the
"Choice of Eternity" as opposed to that "Choice of Life" which the
parable progressively teaches us is irrelevant and pointless, belied
by time and determined by the mad fixations of human fancy. In the
fifty-fourth *Rambler*, a dying man's final hours are described as
"hours of seriousness and wisdom" in which "everything that
terminated this side of the grave was received with coldness and
indifference, and regarded rather in consequence of *the habit of
valuing it*, than from any opinion that it deserved value; it had little
more *prevalence over his mind* than a bubble that was now broken. . . .
All conversation was tedious, that had not a tendency to *dis-engage
him from human affairs*."[68]

Johnson's notorious "fear of death" ties in with his religious
thought concerning "the vacuity of life" through elaborate doctrinal
and existential justification. Ultimately, it is a reassertion of one of
Christianity's main tenets: the idea that a constant contemplation
and remembrance of death is a constant contemplation and
remembrance of the most essential *truth*–a truth which, by pointing
to the urgency which is inherent in temporal life, frees the mind
from its most cherished (and sinful) delusions. The following
passage is a *pensée* of Pascal, but, apart from the language in which
it is couched, it could just as easily have been Johnson's: "La seule
chose qui nous console de nos misères est le divertissement, et
cependant c'est la plus grande de nos misères. Car c'est cela qui
nous empêche principalement de songer à nous et qui nous fait
perdre insensiblement. Sans cela, nous serions dans l'ennui, et cet

---

[68] *Rambler* No. 54, *Works*, II, 260.

ennui nous pousserait à chercher un moyen plus solide d'en sortir. Mais le divertissement nous amuse, et nous fait arriver insensiblement à la mort." [69]

Reaffirming the Stoic-Christian ideal of the contemplation of mortality as a "universal medicine of the mind" (as he calls it in the seventeenth *Rambler*), Johnson gives us the conclusion in which the traditional doctrines, what he himself experienced in his most intimate self and what he took to be the fundamental truth about man, are fused and summed up:

Think, says Epictetus, frequently on poverty, banishment and death, and thou wilt never indulge violent desires, or give up thy heart to mean sentiments. That the maxim of Epictetus is *founded on just observation* will easily be granted, when we reflect, *how that vehemence of eagerness after the common objects of pursuit is kindled in our minds. We represent to ourselves the pleasures of some future possession*, and suffer our thoughts *to dwell attentively upon it, till it has wholly engrossed the imagination*, and permits us not to conceive any happiness but its attainment, or any misery but its loss. [70]

In terms of Johnson the "public figure" such passages are the uninteresting output of a ponderous writer and conversationalist, whose claim to permanence, it is perhaps still felt, lies much more in his acute literary criticism than in any contribution to moral thought. Seen in the context of the anguished man "shut in his den," fully experiencing the "vacuity of life" and battling to achieve godliness against the terrific odds of disease, disorder, and despair and seen in the context of Johnson's elaborate (and highly original) rethinking of the Christian and Humanist heritage, such passages become fascinating moral literature.

[69] Blaise Pascal, *Pensées sur la Religion et sur quelques autres sujets*, ed. L. Lafuma (Paris, 1952), 128– [216–171], "Misère."
[70] *Rambler* No. 17, *Works*, II, 83–4.

CHAPTER TWO: COSMIC HIERARCHY

Qui veut faire l'ange fait la bête

*I*n the following chapter I shall argue that Johnson's satire on man (especially in Rasselas) springs from the view that in human nature reason and passion, the angelic and the bestial, are intermixed in such a way as to modify both and make of them something strictly human. Human intelligence can never be angelic, nor is human passion ever completely animal. The fusion in man of contradictory tendencies makes his nature insufferable to him, and so he seeks to escape it by identifying himself with the idea of an uncompounded existence that is either above or below him. Man's delusion that he can be nonhuman, an angel or a beast, is the supreme manifestation of his escapist, imaginative faculty. In this delusion lies the essence of human irrationality, pride, and folly.

Johnson's attitude toward the idea of man as a middle link in a universal hierarchy of being is best summed up in a paradox. Despite his demonstration that the notion of a universal scale is logically untenable, contradicted by the facts of experience and itself a product of delusive Imagination, his satirical exposé of the human condition depends upon the traditional scheme which placed man between pure intelligence and pure bestiality, sharing characteristics with both but essentially belonging to neither. Like Swift,[1] we shall find Johnson fulfilling his function as a moralist by unmasking man's futile attempt at pure and dispassionate reason (futile because human intelligence is and must be passionate), as well as by ridiculing the primitivist escapism that drives man to idealize nature and to seek the imaginary happiness of a savage or a beast—a happiness that is "imaginary" because the more a savage resembles a

---

[1] The present chapter is a revised version of an article which appeared in *Scripta Hierosolymitana*, XVII, 137–54. I have omitted the extended parallel drawn in that essay between Swift and Johnson since it is based on an interpretation of Swift that now seems to me too simplified.

21

beast the less he resembles a man. Both attempts, we shall see, ultimately come to the same thing in that they represent man's sinful reluctance to exert his *human* reason and so humbly face and accept his mixed nature.

Johnson's rejection of the idea of universal hierarchy in his review of Soame Jenyns's *Free Enquiry into the Nature and Origin of Evil* (1757) is sufficiently well known not to require much elaboration. When the review first appeared in the *Literary Magazine*, it caused such a furor that Johnson was induced to reprint it in a separate small volume, [2] a circumstance attributable not only to the brilliance of his attack but also to the extremely crucial nature of the topic at the time. His argument may be considered under two headings, the one purely philosophical and the other moral-religious, which between them illustrate the paradox I have indicated. The main criticism of the Great Chain of Being in the review—an argument which, as the late Arthur Lovejoy pointed out, "reached very nearly to the root of the matter" [3]—is that the principle of nature's plenitude upon which the entire scheme of a universal ordered hierarchy rests (since the goodness of the Creator is manifest in his desire to "fill" the world by realizing all possible forms of existence, high and low) is not only at odds with observable facts but is self-contradictory as well. The chain of being was supposed to be a a continuous or gradual progression from absolute nonexistence to absolute perfection of existence, but the very idea of such progression, Johnson points out, is unthinkable if one conceives of the universe as "full." The notions of plenitude and hierarchy contradict each other; hence a universe that is both is inconceivable. At each level there must be either a gap or an infinity of intermediate steps. "The highest being not infinite must be . . . at an infinite distance below infinity . . . and in this distance between finite and infinite, there will be room forever for an infinite series of indefinable existence." [4] The same holds true at the bottom of the scale between the lowest form of existence and pure nonexistence. And, in fact, when one thinks of it more closely, "in

[2] See *Works*, VI, 47 n. Pickering notes that this is "a circumstance which appears to have escaped Mr. Boswell's research."

[3] A. O. Lovejoy, *The Great Chain of Being* (Cambridge, Mass., 1950), p. 254. See also P. G. M. C. Hazard, *La pensée européene au XVIIIeme siècle de Montesquieu à Lessing* (Paris, 1946), II, 49; and A. R. Humphries, "The Eternal Fitness of Things, An Aspect of Eighteenth Century Thought," *Modern Language Review*, XLVII (1947).

[4] *A Review of A Free Enquiry*, *Works*, VI, 52.

the scale, wherever it begins or ends, are infinite vacuities. At whatever distance we suppose the next order of beings to be above man, there is room for an intermediate order of beings between them; and if for one order, then for infinite orders; since everything that admits of more or less, and consequently all the parts of that which admits them, may be infinitely divided." [5] Consequently, "no system can be more hypothetical than this, and, perhaps, no hypothesis more absurd." [6] The Great Chain of Being "cannot possibly have being." [7] By showing the way in which the idea of a full scale defies the law of contradiction, Johnson became the only eighteenth-century thinker to show conclusively the weakness of the conception on purely logical grounds.

But for an understanding of Johnson's own view of man's relation to the universe even more important than this exposé of logical inconsistency is the implication, present throughout the review, that the "scale of being is . . . raised by presumptuous imagination." [8] Like all metaphysical "speculation," the theodicy that bases itself on the conception of a universal chain represents for Johnson man's intellectual attempt to rise above himself, to ignore the limiting primacy of his concrete human existence, in which he must be involved to see himself and the world with whatever clarity is allowed him. It is an attempt to see with the eye of an angel or a god by ignoring the objections human reason raises to this single schematic explanation of the universe as to all others. Man's talk of a universal hierarchy is sinful. It is the product of "unprofitable enquiry" and "vain curiosity," [9] "presumptuous" in that it is a symptom of "speculative" human pride and "imaginary" in that it manifests the folly of turning away from what *is* observed by limited human reason.[10]

---

[5] *Ibid.*, p. 53.

[6] *Ibid.*, p. 72.

[7] *Ibid.*, p. 52.

[8] *Ibid.*, p. 59.

[9] Cf., *Diaries*, pp. 383–84 (entry for Aug. 12, 1784): "O Lord, my Maker and Protector, who hast graciously sent me into this world, to work out my salvation . . . while it shall please thee to continue me in this world where much is to be done and little to be known, teach me by thy Holy Spirit to withdraw my Mind from unprofitable and dangerous enquiries, from difficulties vainly curious, and doubts impossible to be solved."

[10] Swift, in his "Digression Concerning the Original, the Use, and Improvement of Madness in a Commonwealth" (*A Tale of a Tub*, sec. IX), undertakes to discover "the faculty of soul" which is responsible for a mere mortal's "taking into

Johnson's criticism of the great chain is thus best understood in terms of the perennial butt of his satire—the tendency to "speculate" which is one of the ways in which man seeks to avoid a rational confrontation and acceptance of his limiting nature. The ridicule Johnson heaps on the facile metaphysics of Jenyns is of the same order as the irony Swift reserves for the flying astronomer-musicians of Laputa and, paradoxically, Pope himself for the impiously proud scientific "speculator" addressed in the *Essay on Man*:

> *Go wondrous creature: mount where Science guides,*
> *Go, measure earth, weigh air, and state the tides;*
> *Instruct the planets in what orbs to run,*
> *Correct old Time, and regulate the Sun,*   (*Epistle, II, ll. 19–22*)

or for the "unconfined" Mad Mathesis of the *Dunciad*, who "to pure Space lifts her ecstatic stare" and "running round the circle finds it square" (IV, 33–34). All these superficially different cases of folly are castigated for what Johnson calls in the review "presumptuous imagination": the pride inherent in all man's intellectual attempts to break through human limitations and so become something that is above him in the great scale.

Johnson is like Swift in that he satirizes this intellectual pride by portraying a man who attempts to soar "into the Empyreal sphere" [11] by literally flying. There is a farcical passage in the Second Book of *Gulliver's Travels* in which little Gulliver, attempting to leap over some Brobdingnagian cow dung, jumps short and finds himself "just in the middle up to [his] knees" (Chap. V). In the Third Book the image of man flying beyond humanity is used as the main satirical device, an eighteenth-century flying version of the traditional Ship of Fools, portrayed with a grotesquerie that rivals

---

his head to advance new systems, with such an eager *zeal*, in things agreed on all hands impossible to be known." Among other examples, he mentions Epicurus, who "modestly hoped that, one time or another, a certain fortuitous concourse of all men's opinions . . . would, by certain clinamina, unite in the notions of atoms and void,"and Descartes, who "reckoned to see, before he died, the sentiments of all philosophers, like so many lesser stars in his romantic system, wrapped and drawn within his own vortex." Such hopes for all-inclusive and absolute systems he calls *imaginations*, and accounts for their origin by the "phenomenon of vapours ascending from the lower faculties to overshadow the brain, and there distilling into conceptions, for which the narrowness of our mother-tongue has not yet assigned any other name beside madness or phrensy." Man's mad attempt at pure rationality, at what is above him, is thus shown with witty precision to originate in his *lower* faculties, and is therefore physiologically demonstrated to be a mark of *bestiality*.

[11] *Essay on Man*, Epistle II. l. 23.

Bosch in its curious mixture of delight, disgust, terror, and farce.[12] But the point of the entire fantasy is precisely what we shall find at the core of Johnson's satire on man. The minds of the Laputans "are so taken up with intense speculations, that they neither can speak nor attend to the discourses of others . . . [they are] so wrapped up in cogitation, that [they are] in manifest danger of falling down every precipice" (Chap. II). They wish to hear, do in fact hear, the music of the spheres—which, as the *Essay on Man* has taught us, is much too "stunning" for mere mortal ears (I, 202). Like Mad Mathesis, they are mathematicians. Like the mad Astronomer whose pathetic story sums up the entire message of *Rasselas*, they are obsessed with the motions of the heavenly bodies, which they calculate with such nicety that "it is in the power of [their] monarch to . . . prevent the falling of dews and rains whenever he pleases" (Chap. II). The Laputans, in short, are satirized for flying beyond the realm of the concretely human, of the "useful" which is the truly rational. One of their eyes turns inward, the other "directly up to the zenith (Chap. II); their inward-turning imagination is thus grotesquely coupled with the upward-turning presumption more generally ridiculed in the image of the flying island they inhabit.

This is precisely what is castigated in the "Dissertation on the Art of Flying" which forms the sixth chapter of *Rasselas*. Johnson is certainly less intensely inventive of grotesque images than Swift (except for such passages as the powerful portrayal of Jenyns's "superior beings" amusing their leisure with "the tossings and contortions of every possible pain" in the review),[13] but *en revanche* his conception of human life is both more compassionate and more tragic (the mad Laputan monarch "prevents the falling of dews and rains" whereas Johnson's mad Astronomer is driven even madder by his anxiety that through some lapse he might neglect to make the rains fall in season). Johnson's flier, like the members of Swift's "academy of modern Bedlam" in the *Tale of a Tub*[14] or the projectors of Lagado in *Gulliver's Travels*,[15] or indeed many of the

---

[12] For a color reproduction of Bosch's "Ship of Fools," now in the Louvre, see C. Linfert, *Hieronymus Bosch, The Paintings, Complete Edition* (London, 1959), Pl. 27.

[13] *Works*, VI, 65.

[14] *A Tale of a Tub* (Everyman Library ed.; New York, 1909.), p. 106.

[15] Bk. III, Chaps. v–vi. Both the Bedlam of the *Tale of a Tub* and Lagado in *Gulliver's Travels* are largely satires on the Royal Society and the canting pride of modern science in general.

virtuosi in the Fourth Book of the *Dunciad*, is "a man eminent for his knowledge of the mechanic powers," who "contrives engines." [16]

It is made clear at the outset that his contraptions are quite "useful" in the twentieth-century utilitarian sense, but quite the reverse of "useful" in the word's older, humanistic connotation. His "hope" of rising above the earth springs from his presumptuous belief that "the fields of air are open to knowledge [and that] only ignorance and idleness need crawl upon the ground" (p. 50). This statement is charged with the irony of its symbolic implications, since in speaking thus of "ignorance and idleness" he reveals his proud and sinful belief in human self-sufficiency. In speaking of "the fields of air" *he* may be referring to literal air, but Johnson means much more than a literal rising of the body from the ground. This becomes clear when the "artist" ecstatically contemplates "with what pleasure a philosopher, furnished with wings, and hovering in the sky, would see the earth, with all its inhabitants, rolling beneath him. . . . How must it amuse the pendent spectator to see the moving scene of land and ocean, cities, and deserts! To survey with equal security the marts of trade, and the fields of battle; mountains infested by barbarians, and fruitful regions gladdened by plenty and lulled by peace" (p. 51). The language Johnson uses here is again charged with his irony: the flier would like to be a "pendent spectator," completely detached from real concern and involvement in the affairs of men—affairs which from his superior position would be seen as merely "amusing." From his imaginary vantage point, peace and war, civilization and savagery, would appear "equal" since he himself would be "secure."

In wishing to rise above the human he manifests the concentration upon Self which is the traditional root of theological Pride. He is criminally deficient in what Johnson found so disturbingly lacking in Jenyns's work—real human commitment; the flier's desire to rise into the "regions of speculation and tranquility" and survey the human scene "with *equal* security" results from his confusion of himself, the man, with a superior order of beings, himself with Pope's divinity "who sees with *equal* eye, as God of all,/A hero perish or a sparrow fall." [17] It is no accident that

---

[16] *Rasselas*, chap. vi, p. 49.
[17] *Essay on Man*, Epistle I, ll. 87–88.

Johnson uses the same image later on when exposing the "wise and happy" stoic of Chapter XVIII, who "from the unshaken throne of rational fortitude, looks down on the scenes of life changing beneath him" (p. 83).

Man's mad and futile attempt to become what is above him in the great scale ultimately is an offense against his human, rational dignity. His dream of a superhuman condition brings out the subhuman that is in him. The objection Rasselas raises against the project of flight is that "every animal has his element assigned him; the birds have the air, and man and beasts the earth" (p. 50). The flier answers that "fishes have the water, in which yet beasts can swim by nature, and men by art" and that flying is merely a kind of swimming in the air. He has "considered the structure of all volant animals and [found] the folding continuity of the bat's wings most easily accommodated to the human form." In other words, in order to "tower into the air beyond the malice and pursuit of man" and to become something higher than man in the scale of existence, he must imitate *the animals* who are below man in that scale; the fact that of all "volant animals" Johnson makes him choose the *bat*, a creature with definitely evil associations, as most "accommodated to the human form" is symbolically meaningful, for Johnson is here "arguing through images" no less than Swift or Pope with their spiders and other "vile" creatures. The point he is making is that man's attempt to escape from himself upwards or downwards in the great chain ultimately comes to the same thing.

What is implicit in the imagery of the "Dissertation on the Art of Flying" becomes entirely explicit in the unmasking of the stoic sage in Chapter XVIII. The chapter reflects the basic structure of the book as a whole and symmetrically repeats the pattern of other constituent episodes in the tale, in that escapist illusion is followed by the human reality which shows up its absurdity. The princess's dream of pastoral bliss is unmasked when she has to endure the company of some extremely unpleasant *real* shepherds. The flier's great plans are exposed when finally, leaping from his stand, he "in an instant dropped into the lake. His wings, which were of no use in the air, sustained him in the water, and the prince drew him to land, half dead with terror and vexation" (p. 53). In the stoic's case, Rasselas hears the impressive discourse of an impressive man. "His look was venerable, his action graceful, his pronunciation clear, and his diction elegant." What he says seems at first to be traditional moral truth expressed in well-turned language, so impressive indeed that it needs someone less innocent than Rasselas to see through the cant and the clichès with which it is ridden. He "showed . . . that when fancy, the parent of passion, usurps the dominion of the mind, nothing ensues but the natural effect of unlawful government,—perturbation and confusion. . . . He compared reason to the sun, of which the light is constant, uniform, and lasting; and fancy to a meteor, of bright but transitory lustre, irregular in its motion, and delusive in its direction" (p. 82).

To a more practiced ear what is wrong with the man before all else is this logorrhea, which points to the split in his consciousness which makes possible pompous self-deception. He sees himself as not really affected by the human predicament and, therefore, denies its reality. This failure in itself sufficiently betrays what in the *Essay on Man* is called "reasoning pride" (I, 123). His basic message is stoical.[18] He "displayed the happiness of those who had obtained the important victory, after which man is no longer the slave of fear, nor the fool of hope." The point is that only a purely spiritual or a purely bestial creature may be free of fear or hope; man by definition is not. In other words, man in his fallen state—the only state with which he is really familiar—must hover between the reason and the passion of which his compounded humanity consists. The stoic is really asserting human self-sufficiency and is denying both religion and morality when he claims that the "important victory" (quite an understatement, this *important!*) of Reason over Passion and its attendant Fancy is possible in the absolute sense and that "this happiness [is] in everyone's power" (p. 83). His blasphemous self-confidence and complacency spring from his blindness to the fact that man is a being who

> *With too much knowledge for the Sceptic side,*
> *With too much weakness for the Stoic's pride,*
> *. . . hangs between.*[19]

[18] In "The Use of Stoical Doctrines in *Rasselas, Chapter XVIII,*" *Modern Language Notes*, LXVIII (Nov., 1953), 439–47, Gwin J. Kolb shows in detail the parallels between the sage's speech and stoic and neo-stoic doctrines. He does not attempt to relate the eighteenth chapter to the pattern and theme of *Rasselas* nor to Johnson's thought in general.

[19] *Essay on Man*, Epistle II, ll. 5–7.

Rasselas is all too ready to accept this "wise and happy" man's presumptuous nonsense for true wisdom. He "could not conceive how any man could reason so forcibly without feeling the cogency of his own arguments." The weight of moral meaning is here carried by the word "feeling." The stoic lacks precisely the quality Johnson found so conspicuously absent from Jenyns's theodicy, real commitment to one's humanity. Of Pope and Jennyns he had said that perhaps they "never *saw* the miseries which they *imagine* thus easy to be borne."[20] In the stoic's case he illustrates the point concretely; Imlac tries to warn the *naif* that teachers of morality like the "wise and happy man" who has impressed him "discourse like angels, but . . . live like men," but Rasselas needs the test of reality to see through this latest of his illusions. When the philosopher's daughter dies the roles are subtly reversed and the unmasking is cruel and final. Rasselas tries to console the bereaved "happy man" with the wisdom he had so recently acquired from him, complacently mouthing the indubitable truth that "mortality is an event by which a man can never be surprised," but the poor stoic rebuffs him with the accusation that he speaks "like one who never *felt* the pangs of separation."

I do not think it has been noticed how closely Chapter XVIII of *Rasselas* parallels Leonato's grieving speech in *Much Ado About Nothing* (V.i.). In fact it seems to me not improbable that Shakespeare's passage provided inspiration for the episode. In the play, when Antonio seeks to console Leonato for Hero's dishonor (which to her father is equivalent to her death), Leonato's answer contains precisely the antistoical point Johnson makes through *the death of his sage's daughter*, and so deserves extensive quotation in this context. Leonato says:

> *I pray thee, cease thy counsel,*
> *Which falls into mine ears as profitless*
> *As water in a sieve: give not me counsel;*
> *Nor let no comforter delight mine ear*
> *But such a one whose wrongs do suit with mine.*
> *Bring me a father that so loved his child,*
> *Whose joy of her is overwhelmed like mine,*
> *And bid him speak of patience . . .*
> *If such a one will smile, and stroke his beard*
> *Bid sorrow wag, cry "hem" when he should groan,*
> *. . . I of him will gather patience.*

[20] *Review of a Free Enquiry, Works* VI, 54–55.

> *But there is no such man: for, brother, men*
> *Can counsel and speak comfort to that grief*
> *Which they themselves not feel; but, tasting it,*
> *Their counsel turns to passion, which before*
> *Would give perceptial medicine to rage,*
> *Fetter strong madness in a silken thread,*
> *Charm ache with air and agony with words:*
> *No, no; 'tis all men's office to speak patience*
> *To those that wring under the load of sorrow,*
> *But no man's virtue nor sufficiency*
> *To be so moral when he shall endure*
> *The like himself. Therefore give me no counsel;*
> *My griefs cry louder than advertisement.*
> ANTONIO: *Therein do men from children nothing differ.*
> LEONATO: *I pray thee, peace*—I will be flesh and blood;
> For there was never yet philosopher
> That could endure the toothache patiently,
> However they have writ the style of gods
> And made a push at chance and sufferance.   (11. 4–38)

Stoic teaching is thus shown up as cant, as a manifestation of the futile pride that will not stand the test of mortal—and therefore passionate—nature. When Johnson's prince parts from the stoic sage, he is "convinced of the emptiness of rhetorical sound, and the inefficacy of polished periods and studied sentences" (p. 84). He has observed at first hand the sterility of the anti-logos which Pope called in the *Dunciad* "the uncreating word"(IV, 653). Canting stoic pride has been exposed as identical with the optimistic pride of the *Free Enquiry:* a product of the imagination that leads man to behave and think as if he were something more than a mere mortal in the order of things. As Pascal, with whose moral thought Johnson's has so much in common, put it: "Ce que les stoïques proposent est si difficile et si vain!" [21]

It should be added that Johnson's attitude toward stoicism is not summed up in the satirical unmasking of its "studied sentences" in *Rasselas.* Inasmuch as stoicism represented a declaration of absolute human self-sufficiency, it offended Johnson's deepest convictions, his very Christianity. But in fact Johnson's Christianity itself has a traditionally stoical strain. Approving quotations from classical Stoic writers abound in his writings[22] and he was apt to quote Epictetus in conversation as well.[23] His defense of the stoic's

[21] *Pensées sur la Religion,* 282– [603–360], p. 183.
[22] E. g., *Rambler* No. 17, *Works,* II, 83–4.
[23] *Life,* V, 279.

anger as against the Epicurean's calm in Lucian's *Jupiter the Tragic*[24] may be merely due to the fact that Lucian's stoic hotly insists on the existence of a divinity whereas the Epicurean complacently denies it, but Johnson's moral thought is in general deeply imbued with a kind of stoicism. Even the false sage in *Rasselas* seems at first to be presenting the typically Johnsonian doctrine of Reason and Imagination, and one does not have to read through many of the *Ramblers* and *Idlers*, or much of *Rasselas* for that matter, to find Johnson arguing for that *other* state of being in which the hopes and fears of the "choice of life" are left behind by means of a rational and virtuous disengagement from the senses, or arguing for a recognition that happiness does not depend on external circumstance since "the fountain of content must spring up in the mind." [25]

The Johnsonian ideal of a tranquil "Choice of Eternity" that is beyond both expectation and disappointment, freed from the tensions of boredom and entertainment, monotony and diversity, indolence and activity, habit and "novelty," is Christian in that it ultimately refers to salvation, but it is stoical in the sense that it depends on a rational disengagement from the world. The difference lies in Johnson's constant insistence that this detachment cannot (and indeed, as we have seen, *must* not) be completely achieved on earth by mere mortals. Again, his position is no different from Pascal's: "[Les] Stoïques . . . concluent qu'on peut toujours ce qu'on peut quelquefois." [26]

This blend of Christian and Stoic, or rather this adaptation of the stoical to the Christian, appears most explicitly in the sixth *Rambler*. The essay opens with the total rejection of stoic precept that underlies the satirical treatment of it we have already encountered in *Rasselas*. "That lofty sect" was committing an "extravagance of philosophy" when it extended the doctrine "that man should never suffer his happiness to depend upon external circumstance" to "an utter exclusion of all corporal pain and pleasure from the regard or attention of a wise man." This is *irrational* because "it is overthrown by the experience of every hour, and the powers of nature rise up against it." As we have seen in *Rasselas*,

<hr>

[24] *Ibid.*, III, 10.
[25] *Rambler* No. 6, *Works*, II, 29.
[26] *Pensées sur la Religion*, 284– [335–350], p. 183.

it does not stand the test of real, observable human life on earth. But though the stoic ideal is more appropriate to angels than to men, "we may very properly inquire, how near to this exalted state it is in our power to approach." "Absolute independence" is nonsense, but surely total dependence on the trivial objects of hope and fear which make up the mass of quotidian life is below the potential dignity of man, who, though fallen and depraved, still hopes for eternal bliss through a return to Grace. Ultimately, therefore, in Johnson's view of man's attempt to rise upward through rational detachment one must distinguish between, on the one hand, the stoic pride that is sinful, presumptuous, and imaginative in its absolute demand, and, on the other, the far from futile attempt to achieve a *human* dignity through the virtuous and religious concentration—inasmuch as it is within the power of frail man to do so—upon higher things.

We have seen how Jenyns's complacent, pseudo-philosophical optimism and the stoicism of irreligious detachment are exposed by Johnson as the attempts of imagination to escape upwards from man's inescapable condition. The Noble Savage myth represents the imagination's attempt to escape it downwards.

The idea that savage life was inherently superior to civilization, and the implication that man could live in a terrestrial paradise if only he could contrive to rid himself of the evil trappings of civilization, was reinforced in the sixteenth and seventeenth centuries by the accounts of travelers to distant lands. Pigafetta, who was in Brazil with Magellan, praised the natives for "following nature" and remarked that their freedom from all the European vices was rewarded with great longevity. Subsequent travelers found the "natural" life of non-Europeans equally admirable.[27] In the eighteenth century, Rousseau's ideas fell on fertile ground, since the notion of the "natural" state was commonly associated on both sides of the Channel with the state of unfallen man, free of the "reasoning pride" that was the bane of civilization.[28] Pope's Indian passage in the *Essay on Man* has a many-faceted, delicate irony, but its rebuke to "civilized" man is still its most obvious function:

[27] See H. N. Fairchild, *The Noble Savage* (New York, 1928).
[28] See H. Roddier, *J. J. Rousseau en Angleterre au XVIIIeme siecle* (Paris, 1950) and R. E. Sewall, "Rousseau's Second Discourse in England from 1775 to 1762," *Philological Quarterly*, XVII (April, 1938), 105–11.

[The Indian's] soul, proud Science never taught to stray
Far as the solar walk, or milky way;
Yet simple Nature to his hope has given,
Behind the cloud-topt hill, an humbler Heaven . . .
To be, contents his natural desire;
He asks no Angel's wing, no Seraph's fire.[29]

It is interesting to note that, in Johnson's violent rejection ("don't cant in defense of savages")[30] of Boswell's suggestions that primitivist ideas might have some validity, the savage is frequently identified with a contemptuous reference to *animals*. When Boswell, evidently having read Bougainville's account of Tahitian prelapsarian happiness, claimed that "the people of Otaheité . . . have the art of navigation," Johnson curtly pointed out that "a dog . . . can swim." When Boswell insisted that "they carve very ingeniously," Johnson countered that "a cat can scratch, and a child with a nail can scratch."[31] The woman who had been living among the Indians and had to be compelled to return to civilization must have been "a speaking cat."[32] In other words, inasmuch as the savage lacks human reason and imagination his capabilities cannot possibly exceed those of other creatures lacking human reason and imagination, creatures below man in the scale of existence; whereas if he does not lack human reason he is no longer a savage.[33]

The controlling image of what is above man and what is below him is no less present in Johnson's remarks on the Noble Savage delusion than in his treatment of the flier in *Rasselas*. When Boswell suggested in another conversation that "there might be some justice in the arguments for the superior happiness of the savage," Johnson's answer was, "Sir, there can be nothing more false. The savages have no bodily advantages beyond those of civilized man . . . and as to care or mental uneasiness, they are not above it, but below it, like bears."[34] Men must suffer the "mental uneasiness" of

---

[29] *Essay on Man*, Epistle I, ll. 101–4, 109–10.

[30] *Life*, IV, 309.

[31] *Ibid.*

[32] *Ibid.*, III, 246. Cf. *Journey to the Hebrides, Life*, V, 78: "A man of any intellectual attainment will not easily go [to America] and immerse himself and his posterity for ages in barbarism," and *Rambler* No. 6, *Works*, II, 27, where Cowley's avowed desire to retire "to some of our American plantations" is described as "chimerical."

[33] Cf. *Life*, III, 49: Even the inhabitants of Otaheité and New Zealand are not in a state of "pure nature," since if they were they would be beasts, not men.

[34] *Life*, II, 73. Cf. *Rambler* No. 128, *Works*, III, 108: "Every part of life has its uneasiness."

hopes and fears which mark their humanity; "dogs," "cats," and "bears" do not. Idealizations of savagery spring precisely from the human desire to be rid of the "uneasiness" which gives man a superiority over the beasts. Only man's cowardly unwillingness to confront rationally his mixed nature drives him to an identification with the unmixed existence that is below him in the great scale.

The "state of nature" of the primitivists is thus no less a hoax of the imagination than the benevolent Nature of deists and theodicists, which Johnson had defined in the *Dictionary* as "an *imaginary* being supposed to preside over the material and animal world." Johnson's own version of the "State of Nature" is close indeed to Hobbes's tough-minded conception. Like Hobbes, who maintained that in the State of Nature "the notions of right and wrong, justice and injustice have . . . no place, . . . no arts; no letters; no society, and, which is worst of all, continual fear and danger of violent death; and the life of man solitary, poor, nasty, brutish, and short," [35] Johnson believed man to be "naturally" immoral, at base a Yahoo: "We are all envious naturally . . . we are all thieves naturally . . . a child always tries to get at what it wants, the nearest way." [36] In another conversation he remarked: "Pity is not natural to man. Children are always cruel. Savages are always cruel. Pity is acquired and improved by the cultivation of reason." [37] Because the hardships of life in nature—the fact that it is all necessity and appetite—make all moral feeling a dangerous luxury, morality cannot be "natural": "had I been an Indian I must have starved, or they would have knocked me on the head, when they saw I could do nothing . . . a savage, when he is hungry, will not carry about with him a looby of nine years old, who cannot help himself. They have no affection, Sir." [38] In September, 1773, Johnson

[35] Thomas Hobbes, *Leviathan or the Matter, Form and Power of a Commonwealth, Ecclesiastical and Civil*, ed. H. Morley (London, 1885), chap. xiii, pp. 64–5. For Johnson, of course, Hobbism was hardly admirable. Of his enemy Hume, for example, he said that he "has no principle. If anything, he is a Hobbist" (*Life*, V, 272).

[36] *Life*, III, 271. In a discussion at Paoli's concerning marriage the General maintained the primitivistic view that "in a state of nature a man and a woman uniting together would form a strong and constant affection, by the mutual pleasure each would receive." Johnson retorted that marriage "is so far from being natural . . . that we find all the motives which they have for remaining in that connection, and the restraints which civilized society imposes to prevent separation, are hardly sufficient to keep them together." *Life*, II, 165.

[37] *Ibid.*, I, 437.

[38] *Ibid.*, IV, 210.

wrote Mrs. Thrale about the island where he was "confined because of bad weather." The "heap of loose stones and turfs" leads him to comment that philosophers who think uncivilized life happy "believe it only while they are saying it." [39] They are guilty of cant in its most reprehensible form.

This is what Johnson meant when he said of Rousseau that "a man who talks nonsense so well, must know that he is talking nonsense." [40] But the nonsense was far from harmless. In preaching what Johnson rightly or wrongly considered total irrationalism, Rousseau was menacing religion, political order, individual morality, art, all human values. "Rousseau, Sir, is a very bad man. I would . . . sign a sentence for his transportation . . . I should like to have him work in the plantations." [41] The devastating satire on the Nature philosopher in *Rasselas* is specifically directed at Rousseau,[42] who had described man in his uncorrupted state as "un être agissant toujours par des principes certains et invariables," a creature possessing

---

[39] *Letters*, I, 329.

[40] *Life*, II, 74. In 1776 Johnson found Lord Monboddo's eccentric primitivism even more absurd than Rousseau's. Rousseau must be aware that what he is suggesting is an intellectual farce and does it to get attention, whereas Monboddo is really stupid enough to take his nature doctrines seriously: "I am afraid (chukling and laughing) Monboddo does *not* know that he is talking nonsense" (*Life*, II, 74). When Johnson had met Monboddo during the Scottish tour of 1773 they disagreed on topics where their disagreement was not surprising, but on the whole seem to have gotten along well enough (Boswell, *Journal of a Tour to the Hebrides, Life*, V, 77–83). Johnson's comment in his Journal was that "the magnetism of Lord Monboddo's conversation drew us out of our way" (*Western Islands*, p. 11, *Life*, V, 74, n. 1). To Mrs. Thrale he wrote that the famous discussion of the relative merits of the shopkeeper and the savage was "maintained on both sides without full conviction: Monboddo declared boldly for the savage, and I perhaps for that reason sided with the citizen" (*Letters*, I, 321). It is difficult to tell whether excessive courtesy or his sense of humor restrained Johnson on this occasion. In the same letter, however, he does make fun of Monboddo's *Of the Origin and Progress of Language* (1733), in which Darwinian theories are prefigured. To Johnson, this is "a strange book." Monboddo reacted with less amusement: Johnson was "the most invidious and malignant man [he had] ever known" (quoted in *Life*, II, 74 n. 1).

[41] *Ibid.*, II, 12. There was only one occasion on which Johnson approved of a passage in Rousseau, when he agreed with Mrs. Thrale that Rousseau's comment on "the hard Task of Christianity" was "beautiful" (*Thraliana*, I, 203–4). Chester F. Chapin, in "Dr. Johnson's Approval of a Passage in Rousseau, "*Notes and Queries*" (Nov., 1959), 413–14, locates the passage referred to as *La Nouvelle Héloise*, Part VI, Letter 6: "la véritable humilité du Chretien . . . c'est de trouver toujours sa tâche au dessus de ses forces, etc." (ed. Daniel Mornet [Paris, 1925], IV, 224–5).

[42] See Roddier, *J. J. Rousseau*, pp. 49–52, "Rousseau est-il visé en Rasselas," and Sewall, "Rousseau's Second Discourse," pp. 105–11.

"une céleste et majestueuse simplicité dont son Auteur l'avoit empreintè," [43] "La Nature," he pointed out in the *Second Discours,*

traite tous les animaux abandoné à ses soins avec une prédilection, qui semble montrer combien elle est jalouse de ce droit . . . . Le Cheval, le Chat, le Taureau, l'Ane même ont la plupart une taille plus haute, tous une constitution plus robust . . . dans les forets que dans nos maisons. Il en est ainsi de l'homme même: en devenant sociable et Esclave, il devient foible, craintif, rampant.[44]

In the concluding paragraph of the *Premier Discours* Rousseau cried out:

O vertu, science sublime des ames Simples: faut il donc tant de peines et d'appareil pour te connoître. Tes principes ne sont il pas gravés dans tous les coeurs? Et ne suffit-il pas, pour apprendre tes lois, de rentrer en soi-meme, et d'écouter la voix de la conscience dans le silence des passions? Voila la véritable philosophie; sachons nous en contenter.[45]

Johnson appears to be parodying these passages point by point in the Nature philosopher's impassioned speech. The way to be happy, says this sage, is

to live according to nature, in obedience to that universal and unalterable law with which every heart is originally impressed; which is not written on it by precept, but engraved by destiny, not instilled by education, but infused at our nativity. He that lives according to nature will suffer nothing from the delusions of hope, or importunities of desire. . . . Other men may amuse themselves with subtle definitions or intricate ratiocinations. Let them learn to be wise by easier means: let them observe the hind of the forest, and the linnet of the grove.[46]

The Nature philosopher's cure for the "uneasiness" that Johnson saw as the real difference between man and "the hind of the forest" thus makes him as absurd as the "wise and happy man" of Chapter XVIII.[47] The Nature philosopher's remedy lies in the animal nature that is below man rather than in the purely rational that is above, but

[43] Jean Jacques Rousseau, *Second Discours* (Amsterdam, 1755), lv., quoted in Sewall, "Rousseau's Second Discourse."

[44] *Ibid.,* p. 25.

[45] *Oeuvres* (Neuchatel, 1764), I, 57.

[46] *Rasselas,* chap. xxii, p. 91. M. J. Quinlan suggests that Johnson intends to satirize not Rousseau but Shaftesbury, Richard Cumberland, and Samuel Clarke. *Samuel Johnson, A Layman's Religion* (Madison, 1964), p. 35. But for Johnson, Rousseau was much guiltier of deifying Nature than writers like Clarke.

[47] There was in fact a strong strain of both cultural and chronological primitivism in the teaching of the Roman Stoics. For passages from Seneca amply illustrating this tendency see A. O. Lovejoy *et al., A. Documentary History of Primitivism and Related Ideas,* (Baltimore, 1935), I, pp. 260–87.

the difference between the two sages is superficial. Both insist that man can be "happy" by ridding himself of his burdensome humanity. When Rasselas humbly remarks that he "doubts not the truth of a position which a man so learned has so confidently advanced" and only inquires "what it is to live according to nature," the philosopher's canting reply is that "to live according to nature, is to act always with due regard to the fitness arising from the relations and qualities of causes and effects; to concur with the great and unchangeable scheme of universal felicity; to co-operate with the general disposition and tendency of the present system of things." This makes his point quite identical with the optimistic one satirized in the review of *A Free Enquiry*.

What Johnson is objecting to in Rousseau and in his English adherents becomes clear when we note that the Nature philosopher's discourse is made in answer to "one who *appeared more affected*" than the rest of those present, by Rasselas' narrative of a hermit who hated the life he had deliberately chosen. This person who is deeply moved explains the hermit's dilemma in terms of what Mrs. Thrale had called Johnson's "favourite hypothesis," [48] and which is in fact the chief theme of *Rasselas*. "The hope of happiness," he says, "is so strongly impressed, that the longest experience is not able to efface it. Of the present state, whatever it be, we feel, and are forced to confess, the misery; yet, when the same state is again at a distance, imagination paints it as desirable." [49] What is wrong with the Nature philosopher, in other words, is that he is not "affected" by the one great truth real experience is capable of showing beyond doubt: that human life *sui generis*, because of its "middle" nature, must involve misery and frustration. Rousseau's doctrines are for Johnson pure "nonsense" because they appear to cover up this basic fact in a mass of verbiage that can mean only one more example of the triumph of imagination and self-deception. What Johnson finds missing in such "speculations" is once again the direct confrontation and rational acceptance of human reality.

It is this obstinate insistence on experience, and in particular on the experience of life as "a pill which none of us can bear to swallow without gilding," [50] that forms the basis of all Johnson's

---

[48] *Thraliana*, 179.

[49] *Rasselas*, chap. xxii, p. 90–91.

[50] Mrs. Thrale, *Anecdotes*, in *J. M.*, I, 204. Johnson is arguing that one must be charitable to beggars despite the fact that in all probability the money will be spent on gin and tobacco. Cf. *Thraliana*, I, 180.

violent, ironic, and often insulting attacks, in both his conversation and writings, upon all those whom he considered cowardly and hypocritical in that they would not admit and face life's "misery." Once, during a conversation about drunkenness, Mrs. Anna Williams wondered "what pleasure men can take in making *beasts* of themselves." Johnson's response to the stimulus was immediate: "I wonder, Madam, that you have not penetration enough to see the strong inducement of this excess; for he who makes a *beast* of himself gets rid of *the pain of being a man.*" [51] In his own writings he did not hesitate to describe "the dismal receptacles to which the prostitute returns from her nocturnal excursions . . . the wretches that lie crowded together, mad with intemperance, ghastly with famine, nauseous with filth, and noisome with disease." [52] He was irritated by the mention of the very possibility of absolute happiness and serenity on earth, for he regarded such talk as inevitably a combination of complacency, hypocrisy, and irreligion. Mrs. Thrale relates how a friend once insisted that "his wife's sister was *really* happy, and called upon the lady to confirm his assertion." When the lady did so "somewhat roundly," Johnson's irritated comment was that if she really was as contented as she claimed to be, "her life gives the lie to every research of humanity; for she is happy without health, without beauty and without understanding." Later to the reproving Mrs. Thrale, he said, "I tell you, the woman is ugly, and sickly, and foolish, and poor; and would it not make a man *hang* himself to hear such a creature say, it was happy?" [53]

Thus human life is defined by the need it creates for narcotics of one kind or another. I have tried to explain the connection Johnson sees between some of the philosophical narcotics he exposes in his satire on man. The optimist, the stoic, and the primitivist[54]— all avoiding confrontation of the real misery of fallen man, all claiming to possess the secret of "happiness" on earth—are unmasked as intellectual drug-peddlers. The internal coherence of this pessimistic exposé, I have argued, becomes clearer when we are

[51] Rev. Percival Stockdale, *Anecdotes,* in *J.M.,* II, 333.
[52] *Rambler* No. 71, *Works,* III, 308.
[53] Mrs. Thrale, *Anecdotes,* in *J.M.,* II, 335.
[54] It should perhaps be remarked that although Johnson's dislike for primitivistic ideas must ultimately be traced to his orthodoxy, Christianity itself was not exempt from a traditional primitivistic bias. For an admirably detailed study of primitivism in patristic and medieval thought see G. Boas, *Essays on Primitivism and Related Ideas in the Middle Ages* (Baltimore, 1948).

aware of the paradoxical role played in Johnson's thought by the conception of man as middle link in a universal hierarchy. Man has two faculties. His Reason discloses the human situation as it is; his Imagination avoids or "gilds" it. The chain of being, itself the drug of optimists and theodicists, is to be rejected as a hoax of the imagination since it is nothing but a way of sweetening the pill with lofty verbiage, but it nevertheless forms the metaphorical framework within which Johnson's view of both man's rationality and of his escapist fantasies becomes clear. Man in reason knows himself for what he is; in imagination he tries to become an angel, a beast, or, unwittingly, both at once. The more he does so, the more manifest are his real misery and, by negation, the potential rationality—the possibility of virtue and dignity—implied in his mixed nature.

Johnson's metaphysical position can only be summed up in this paradox. R. K. Kaul, who concludes on entirely insufficient evidence that "according to Johnson there are three kinds of creation, in the ascending order, the mechanical, the sensitive and the rational" [55] misses the point. His statement, which would ascribe to Johnson actual belief in a cosmic hierarchy, is misleading because, in the first place, Johnson never said this, and, secondly, for him to have said it would have put him on a level with the metaphysical "speculators" he despised. Kaul's assertion is based on a single sentence of the Sophist (not "Skeptic" as Kaul erroneously labels him) satirized in the ninty-fifth *Rambler:* "I sometimes exalted vegetables to sense, and sometimes degraded animals to mechanism." A reading of this assertion in its context shows that Johnson was not expressing his own metaphysical credo at all; he was merely illustrating his protagonist's "vitiated, ignorant and heady" pride in his ability to "distinguish [himself] by sophisms." [56]

I hope I have shown more accurately what role the idea of metaphysical hierarchy actually played in Johnson's thought. For all his lambasting of Jenyns and Pope, for all his assertion that "the chain of being cannot possibly have being," his satirical exposé itself depends on the concept it attacks. Plenitude and hierarchy do not make sense, but the concomitants of the chain concept—that

[55] "Dr. Johnson on Matter and Mind," *Johnsonian Studies*, ed. M. Wahba (Cairo, 1962), p. 104.
[56] *Works*, II, 451.

man is best understood in terms of his attempt to become what is above him or what is below him, and that the exercise of human reason is at its noblest not when it is abstract and detached but when it is truly "passionate"—are at the core of everything Johnson had to say about life.

CHAPTER THREE: THE ART OF
FORGETFULNESS

*M*emory, in Johnson's thought, may be seen as the temporal inverse of hope or desire or expectation. Human expectation represents the mind's tragic transcendence of the present moment toward future objects that are in themselves neutral but which it transmutes into goals of pursuit. We are "condemn'd to Hope's *delusive* mine/as on we toil from day to day"[1] because the dissatisfaction inherent in our present circumstances drives us to project our wishes into the future, fixing upon some object which we imaginatively transform into a solution of all ills. Such objects are necessarily vain and illusory[2] because the temporal process itself belies our idealization: when once the imagined future has emerged into the actual present, that is to say is no longer *distant* in time, it by definition is no longer ideal. Being temporal, the objects of expectation are elusive; our hope is frustrated by the materialization of its object, so that the mind must once again "send imagination out upon the wing"[3] in new plans and desires. What is true of hope is inversely true of memory. Like our "expectations," our memories (as distinct from "recollections" which are merely the calling to consciousness of stored information)[4] represent a transcendence of time through the mind's projection into the past in search of unattainably infinite satisfaction.

Expectation and retrospection are the forward and backward projections of *Imagination*, the key term of the Johnsonian ethos. All of Johnson's general observations on the human condition and all of

---

[1] *On the Death of Dr. Robert Levet*, ll. 1–2.
[2] This is the central theme of both *Rasselas* and *The Vanity of Human Wishes*.
[3] *Rasselas*, chap. xliv, p. 140.
[4] To recollect means "to recover to memory" (*Dictionary*). I do not wish to imply, however, that Johnson consistently uses "memory" to designate imaginative projection and "recollection" to denote the technical operation of the mind when it turns to stored experience. As in most other cases, Johnson does not keep to fixed labels. He uses interchangeably all terms that in ordinary usage are synonymous or nearly so.

his particular observations on the various phenomena of human life are ultimately explicable in terms of the basic tension he sees between the rational and the imaginative faculties of man. What Johnson meant by Imagination may be understood in terms of his frequent discussion of the incompatibility between the mental and the bodily modes of existence. The starting point is the fact that the body must obey the restrictions placed upon it by time, whereas the mind is unrestricted: the body has no existence apart from its *present* being, whereas the mind's mode of existence lies precisely in its constant projection of itself into future or past. The consequence of this difference in the modes of being of body and of mind is a perpetual incompatibility between human conceptions and human performance. The body can never entirely keep up with the mind. Imagination may thus be defined as the mental faculty which tends to increase this incompatibility, Reason as the mental faculty which tends to diminish it. When the mind loses touch with the actual possibilities of performance represented by the body's purely temporal mode of being, Imagination may be said to hold full sway, for this is the condition of overt madness. On the other hand, a life led with the constant end of decreasing the incompatibility between human transcendence and human actuality is the rational life, or, interchangeably, the sane and virtuous life, in that it implies a confrontation of one's true state. In the conclusion of the Seventeenth *Rambler*, for example, an essay devoted to the contemplation of mortality (and one of Johnson's most impressive performances), we are told that "it is always pleasing to observe, how much more our minds can conceive, than our bodies can perform; yet *it is our duty, while we continue in this complicated state, to regulate one part of our composition by some regard to the other*." [5]

In the *Dictionary*, Imagination is defined as (among other things) "the power of forming *ideal* pictures" or "the power of representing things *absent*." In both expectation and retrospection we "indulge the power of fiction," as Imlac puts it,[6] and employ our fundamental irrationality to supply us with "objects of attention" that are idealized, "gilded," and distorted in accordance with the mind's infinite need. The indulgence of such memory will be observed, of

[5] *Rambler* No. 17, *Works*, II, 87. The entire essay may serve as an illustration of the points I have been making.

[6] In his crucial analysis of "The Dangerous Prevalence of Imagination," *Rasselas*, chap. xliv, p. 140.

course, most strikingly in cases where present and future no longer hold much in store for "the attention," as "when we are old [and] *amuse the langour of age* with the recollection of youthful pleasures" [7] (which at the time were quite unreal, since they were dependent on "expectation"). But imaginative memory, the mind's leap from the present moment into the seemingly satisfying past, may occur throughout life whenever we are "offended by the bitterness of truth." [8] "He to whom the present offers nothing will often be looking backward into the past." [9] In fact, this power of "forming ideal pictures" is constantly at work upon the past, even when we are not completely aware of it, for it is our most spontaneous reaction to the elusiveness of experience. Our natural need to stop time, to rest in an immutable X that will not slip through our fingers, leads us to idealize scenes of the past in precisely the way we imaginatively transform the future "prospects" of expectation into seemingly absolute satisfactions. The discrepancy between the real setting of our past experience and what we have imaginatively made of it by our restless craving for the ideal was what Johnson had in mind when he sadly told Baretti how he "went down to [his] native town, where [he] found the streets narrower and shorter than [he] *thought* [he] had left them." [10]

Like all his basic ideas, Johnson's observation of the fallacies and distortions of memory becomes highly generalized and manifold. It underlies his distrust of the philosophical glorification of primitive states, the romantic glorification of mindless childhood, the primitivistic exaltation of precivilized, supposedly prelapsarian man, and the notion of a golden age of one kind or another which Johnson observed to be a perennial human obsession. Ultimately, it may be seen to underly his distrust of any kind of idealized, "happy" literature, notably his antipathy toward pastoral poetry or toward the theodicies of philosophical optimism. The function of the true poet (or, interchangeably, of the true moralist) is to expose the "luscious falsehoods" which the mind creates "whenever she is offended with the bitterness of truth," [11] to present not the "ideal pictures" of

---

[7] *On Shakespeare*, p. 78. The phrase recurs in Johnson's writings. Cf., e.g., *Rambler* No. 90, *Works*, II, 421: "the langours of attention."
[8] *Rasselas*, chap. xliv, p. 140.
[9] *Idler* No. 72, *Works*, IV, 365.
[10] *Letters*, I, 139–40.
[11] *Rasselas*, chap. xliv, p. 140.

imaginative memory and hope but the true pictures which Reason sees in the nature of things. Johnson's entire work, whether literary, scholarly, religious, or political, may be seen as an attempt to do precisely that.

Man's passion becomes his obsessive dream. The object of his passion, whether the future object of desire or the past object of memory, in extreme states rules out attention to all else, becoming an imaginative absolute which subjectively appears to have a validity beyond time. Perhaps the most striking example of such obsessive retrospection in Johnson's writings is presented in *Rasselas* in the chapters that deal with the Princess' reaction to the loss of her beloved Pekuah. She is described as having "sat from morning to evening recollecting all that had been done or said by her Pekuah, *treasured up with care* every trifle on which Pekuah had set an accidental value, and which might recall to mind any little incident or careless conversation. The sentiments of her whom she now *expected to see no more*, were *treasured in her memory as rules of life*." [12]

"Treasured in her memory": such hoarding of particulars is dangerous both because the particulars themselves undergo Imagination's process of distortion and because they leave no room for attention to matters at hand or to the future objectives that guarantee the forward movement of life. What Imlac says of the general "Prevalence of Imagination"—"the mind, in weariness or leisure, *recurs constantly* to the favourite conception" [13]—is thus true of obsessive retrospection no less than of obsessive expectation: the Princess' mind, "though forced into short excursions, always *recurred to the image of her friend*." [14] Her "hunger of imagination" has taught her to feed upon this particular image from the past, so that no present experience and no projection into future experience can provide the same satisfaction. As we learn in the Seventy-fifth *Idler*, "if the repositories of thought are already full, what can they receive? If the mind is *employed on the past or future*," it cannot attend to the present. In order "to attend" to life, in order to move through time with relative sanity, we must minimize the discrepancy between our conceptions and our actuality; we must retain our rational control of both desire and memory, be "able, at pleasure, to evacuate

[12] *Ibid.*, chap. xxxv, p. 118.
[13] *Ibid.*, chap. xliv, p. 140.
[14] *Ibid.*, chap. xxxv, p. 119.

[our] mind" and bring to our pursuits "an intellect defecated and pure, neither turbid with care, nor agitated by pleasure." [15]

I have tried to show how Johnson sees in the dangers of memory the corollary of the dangers of earthly hopes or wishes. In hope future objects are imaginatively idealized until they appear infinitely desirable; in obsessive memory the same thing happens to experiences of the past. But hope is not the only way in which the mind throws itself into the future. Throughout Johnson's writings, as indeed throughout the moral and psychological literature he read,[16] hope is nearly always coupled with *fear*. "The hopes and *fears* of this world," [17] "the fears and hopes . . . of this life," [18] are what menace balance, rationality, and piety. In *The Vanity of Human Wishes*, we are invited to see how "hope and fear, desire and hate/ O'erspread with snares the clouded maze of fate" (5–6). Hope is complemented by fear because fear is in reality negative hope. What we fear we hope to avoid, just as what we desire we fear we may not attain. In both cases illusion is involved, the objects of both earthly hope and earthly fear being what Hazlitt called "bugbears and idols." [19] "As treach'rous phantoms in the mist delude/ [Man] shuns *fancied* ills, or chases *airy* good":[20] the relation between hope and fear is not merely schematic; hope itself *is* a kind of fear, since what Johnson has in mind is the general anxiety or "uneasiness" [21] which characterize all expectation, all projections into the future, whether of the "chasing" or of the "shunning" kind. Hope and fear are interchangeable in the sense that they both sum up the tragic restlessness inherent in man's temporal being, his mind's constant over-reaching of his body.

Precisely the same holds true of memory. The mind turns to the past in search of absolute satisfaction, painting past experience with the colors of infinity, and is haunted by "fearful" memories that are no less obsessive. The very transformation of past experience into obsessions implies a kind of misery which is analogous to fear. When Imlac shows how the "prevalence of imagination" makes life "pass

---

[15] *Idler* No. 75, *Works*, IV, 370.

[16] E.g., Burton's *Anatomy of Melancholy*

[17] *Diaries*, p. 78.

[18] *Ibid.*, p. 103.

[19] *Collected Works of William Hazlitt* (London, 1914), XI, 557.

[20] *Vanity of Human Wishes*, ll. 9–10.

[21] Cf. *Life*, II, 73: "as to care or *mental uneasiness*, [savages] are not above it, but below it, like bears."

in *dreams of rapture or anguish"* [22] he is referring to the mind's
transcendence both in the "hopes and fears" that feed upon an
imagined future and in the obsessively pleasurable or horrifying
memories of an imagined past.

This is where Johnson's basic psychological insight into the
human predisposition toward *guilt* becomes relevant. Imagination in
general is seen by Johnson as spurred and intensified by our tendency
to take upon ourselves responsibility for what in reason we would
see to be outside our power. The Astronomer, for example, whose
imagination has so far gained control over his reason as to make him
believe that he has power over the weather, is very anxious that his
tremendous duties will not be discharged perfectly and catastrophe
will ensue. His unconscious megalomania (which is an extreme
symbol of the general human "prevalence of imagination") is "a
disease of imagination which is *complicated with the dread of guilt,*" an
irrational condition in which *"fancy and conscience . . . act
interchangeably."* [23] The same thing happens in the retrospective
obsessions which we have seen to be analogous to hope and fear.
Our potential of anxiety, our natural propensity to feel guilt and
irrationally to employ our conscience upon evils that are really not
of our making, is particularly exercised when calamities befall persons
who are close to us. After her favorite had been kidnapped,
Nekayah blames herself for what is really not her fault, and it takes
considerable persuasion on the part of Imlac (who, representing the
point of view of Reason, becomes a kind of therapist in this case)
to lessen the harmful effects of her overdeveloped sense of guilt.
"Fancy" and "conscience" do indeed act interchangeably in her case:
even after Imlac has practiced his rational therapy upon her, we find
her *"imagining* many expedients by which the loss of Pekuah might
have been prevented." [24] And it should be emphasized that Johnson,
here as elsewhere in *Rasselas,* is exposing and analysing what he
considers average, "normal" humanity—*us,* in other words—since,
as we learn in Imlac's "Prevalence of Imagination" discourse, all
apparent normality conceals a latent madness that is the mark of
fallen humanity.

[22] *Rasselas,* chap. xliv., p. 141.
[23] *Ibid.*
[24] *Ibid.,* chap. xxxiv, p. 115.

Obsessive states of sorrow, intensified by "the pangs of guilt," are dangerous in that the fixation upon the past interferes with the "regulated" state that is our precarious normality by increasing the discrepancy between our idealizing conceptions and our temporal actuality. Nekayah, completely obsessed with Pekuah's loss, resolves "to retire from the world with all its flatteries and deceits . . . till with a mind purified from all earthly desires [she will] enter that state to which all are hastening, and in which [she hopes] again to enjoy the friendship of Pekuah." [25] The irony here is subtle. It would appear at first that Nekayah has been driven to true piety by her loss. Such, indeed, is Johnson's traditional notion of the "use" of calamities and his explanation of the evils of life: they serve to disillusion us with the "Choice of Life" and drive us to the rational "Choice of Eternity." But, in fact, Nekayah's rejection of earthly delusions is in terms of one particular delusion, in terms of her fixation upon one idealized point in the past which not her reason but her *imagination*, complicated with guilt, characteristically focussing all intensity and all value upon a particular to the exclusion of all else, has given the dignity of a transcendental absolute. Her conception of the afterlife is in essence an epitome of earthly obsession, of a vain human wish. Her idea of Paradise is now identical with her idea of Pekuah, just as it had previously been (and later once again becomes) connected with her favorite wish-fulfillment of pastoral bliss. Her decision to reject the world is rightly seen by Imlac as a manifestation of the irrational and dangerous human need to *stop time*. "Do not entangle your mind by *irrevocable determinations* . . . you will wish to return to the world when *the image of your companion has left your thoughts*," he says. " 'That time,' said Nekayah, 'will never come.' " [26]

I do not think it has been sufficiently noticed how strongly the chapters that trace Nekayah's grief in *Rasselas* reflect Johnson's personal experiences at the time. *Rasselas* was written for the express purpose of defraying the expense of his mother's funeral,[27] to whom he was strongly attached. He was so "extremely agitated" [28] by his mother's death that he was "afraid of being left alone." [29] The fear, as

[25] *Ibid.*, chap. xxxv, p. 119.
[26] *Ibid.*, p. 120.
[27] *Life*, I, 341.
[28] *Life*, II, 124.
[29] *Letters*, I, 125.

always, was the terror of incipient madness, and he "composed his mind" only by an extraordinary effort of will.[30] Guilt was a strong element in his agitation. Boswell recounts how he "regretted much his not having gone to visit his mother for several years, previous to her death." [31] In Johnson's last letter to his mother he begs to be forgiven for "all that I have done ill, and all that I have omitted to do well." [32] Shortly after her death Johnson wrote Lucy Porter that if his mother were to live again "surely I should behave better to her. But she is happy, and what is past is nothing to her; and for me, since I cannot repair my faults to her, I hope repentance will efface them." [33] In the *Idler* of January 27, 1759, obviously written under the impact of his bereavement, Johnson writes that "the loss of a friend *upon whom the heart was fixed*, to whom *every wish and endeavour tended*, is a state of dreary desolation, in which the mind looks abroad impatient of itself, and finds nothing but emptiness and horror." [34] The language of this paper is extremely reminiscent of Nekayah's "grieving and musing" in *Rasselas*.[35] That Johnson regarded his extreme grief as a dangerous compound of imagination and guilt which was a threat to sanity becomes clear when we find him in his Prayer of January 23, 1758 "returning thanks for the alleviation of [his] sorrow." [36] The threat, as with Nekayah, had ultimately been that of criminal despair. "Forgive me, O Lord," prays Johnson, "whatever my Mother has suffered by my fault, whatever I have done amiss, and whatever duty I have neglected. *Let me not sink into useless dejection.*" [37] Nekayah, "when she saw nothing more to be tried, sunk down inconsolable *in hopeless dejection.*" [38]

The danger of obsessive grief is the danger of the kind of despair which is in itself a denial not only of earthly hope but also of otherworldly hope, and therefore of religion itself. Johnson

[30] *Life*, II, 124.
[31] *Life*, I, 340.
[32] *Letters*, I, 121.
[33] *Letters*, I, 124.
[34] *Idler* No. 41, *Works*, IV, 271.
[35] E.g. (*ibid.*, p. 272): "Happiness is not found in self-contemplation; it is perceived only when reflected from another." Nekayah similarly comments that "since Pekuah was taken from her . . . [she lacks] *the radical principle of happiness,*" for she has "no one to love or trust" (*Rasselas*, chap. xxxv, p. 120).
[36] *Diaries*, p. 67.
[37] *Ibid.*, p. 69.
[38] *Rasselas*, chap. xxxiv, p. 117.

was hardly the first to connect the effects of "tender conscience" and "aroused imagination" with the threat of religious despair.[39] His conception of "profitable" sorrow, of the kind of rational mourning which turns our thoughts toward God, implies an emotional tightrope over an abyss of obsession and of mad grief that would halt time in order to perpetuate itself. This is perhaps brought out most clearly in the prayers written in 1752 after the death of his beloved Tetty: "And now, O Lord, release me from my sorrow . . . and enable me to do my duty . . . without disturbance from *fruitless grief, or tumultuous imaginations.*"[40] In May he was repeating the same prayer: "O Lord grant . . . that I may not sorrow *as one without hope,* but may now return to the duties of my present state . . . nor idleness lay me open to *vain imaginations.*" [41] Four years later (March 28, 1756), he was still beseeching God "that *the remembrance of my Wife . . . may not load my soul with unprofitable sorrow.*"[42]

"The state of mind oppressed with a sudden calamity," says Imlac, "is like that of the fabulous inhabitants of the new-created earth, who when the first night came upon them, supposed the day would never return." [43] But day does return, and it is our religious and moral duty to behave in accordance with this fact. "The business of life is to go forwards," [44] we are told in the Seventy-second *Idler.* "We must be busy about good and evil," exhorts *Idler* No. 73,[45] for virtue implies the rational exercise of choice in terms of present actualities. The obsessions of memory are even more dangerous to reason and virtue than the futile fixations of hope and fear, because "he who sees evil in prospect meets it in his ways; but he who catches it by retrospection *turns back to find it.*" [46]

It is this acute consciousness of the psychological dangers of retrospection that explains Johnson's recommendation, in more than one of his moral writings, that we cultivate "the art of forgetfulness." In the forty-fifth *Idler* he identifies himself with

[39] For references and a discussion of the traditional connection made among imagination, overscrupulous conscience, and despair, see my essay "Religious Despair in Mediaeval Literature and Art," *Mediaeval Studies,* XXVI (1964), 231–56.

[40] *Diaries,* p. 46.

[41] *Ibid.,* p. 47.

[42] *Ibid.,* p. 61.

[43] *Rasselas,* chap. xxxv, p. 120.

[44] *Idler* No. 72, *Works,* IV, 363.

[45] *Idler* No. 73, *Works,* IV, 365.

[46] *Idler* No. 72, *Works,* IV, 363.

Themistocles who "when an offer was made to [him] of teaching him the art of memory . . . answered that he would rather wish for the art of forgetfulness. He felt his *imagination haunted by phantoms of misery which he was unable to suppress,* and would gladly have calmed his thoughts with an oblivious antidote." [47] In the seventy-second *Idler* Johnson elaborates the idea that "it would add much to human happiness, if an art could be taught of forgetting all of which the remembrance is at once useless and afflictive." [48] "Forgetfulness is necessary to remembrance"[49] because the thoughts that are merely afflictive in their combination of scrupulosity and obsessiveness take up that room in the mind which should be open to recollection useful to the business we have at hand and are, therefore, an impediment to both action and sanity. The criterion of Reason, here as throughout Johnson's writings, is that of control or regulation. "Forgetfulness" implies a regulating power over impulse. Just as Imlac argues that "there is no man who is entirely master of his imagination, *no man whose ideas will come and go at his command,*" [50] but that we must strive by sheer will power and lucidity to attain a rational control of our fancies, so in the Seventy-second *Idler* we learn that "the power of forgetting is capable of improvement. Reason will, by a resolute contest, prevail over imagination." [51]

But the "art of forgetfulness" is the true "art of memory" in a more basic sense. Imagination in the Johnsonian ethos is ultimately that power in man which blinds him to his true state and is therefore the supreme menace to his salvation. Salvation itself is the state of our forgetfulness or control of irrational impulses, of our "letting go from the remembrance" [52] all the earthly obsessions which distract our attention from the true urgency of our mortal lives. All of Johnson's thoughts ultimately point to what he considers *rational* memory, the *memento mori* which is identical with

---

[47] *Idler* No. 45, *Works*, IV, 281. Cf., George Wither's *Abuses, Stript and Whipt* (London, 1614), I, 11: "Monstrous shapes which seem for to appear/Through [despairing mens'] *imaginations.*" Examples could be multiplied from the hortatory and allegorical literature of the Middle Ages and the Reformation with which Johnson was familiar.
[48] *Idler* No. 72, *Works*, IV, 364.
[49] *Ibid.*, p. 363.
[50] *Rasselas*, chap. xliv, p. 140.
[51] *Idler* No. 72, *Works*, IV, 364.
[52] This is one of the meanings of "forget" as Johnson defines it in his *Dictionary*.

the *memento quod es homo*. "Let me *remember* [that] of the short life of man a great part is already past," [53] he prays year after year. "Make me *remember*, O God, that every day is thy gift";[54] "make me remember how much every day brings me closer to the grave." [55] The beautiful or monstrous idealizations of fancy and passion stop time for us and make us avoid and escape remembrance of our true state. All the operations of Reason ultimately depend on the essential "remembrance of death [which] ought to predominate in our minds, as an habitual and settled principle, always operating, though not always perceived . . . *our attention should seldom wander . . . from our own condition*." [56] Johnson, whether asking God to make him "forget" his guilt-ridden sorrows, to "remember" the urgency of his true condition, or to be "animated with reasonable hope," [57] is ultimately praying for the same thing—for what could interchangeably be termed sanity, rationality, or the redemption of his immortal soul.

[53] *Diaries*, p. 110.
[54] *Ibid.*, p. 49.
[55] *Ibid.*, p. 65.
[56] *Rambler* No. 78, *Works* II, 368.
[57] *Diaries*, p. 74.

CHAPTER FOUR: IDLE SOLITUDE AND DIABOLICAL IMAGINATION

*I*t *has recently been shown that eighteenth-century writers were preoccupied more than those of perhaps any other century with the arguments for and against solitary retreat.*[1] One argument commonly put forth was an identification of the virtuous social life with rationality and retreat into solitude with vicious irrationality, but much of the literature of the age is imbued with an opposite strain, a glorification of solitude which frequently finds expression in imitations of such works as Horace's second Epode ("Beatus ille") and Virgil's second Georgic ("O fortunatus nimium"). As the century progressed this note became stronger, culminating in Rousseau's prophecy of romantic subjectivism: "Cherchez la solitude, voila d'abord tout le secret." [2]

In his general condemnation of solitude Johnson was, as always, at one with the orthodox values threatened by the increasing romanticism of his age. In the present chapter I shall attempt to view the connection Johnson habitually made between solitude and the sin of sloth in the light of that tradition and in terms of the polarity of faculties to which he referred all human experience, that of saving Reason and damning Imagination. In addition, by surveying some of Johnson's many comments on the way Imagination "erupts" in solitude, we should be able to go deeper into the meaning of this crucial concept.

Solitude and sloth, Johnson felt, could be equated because in both lay the greatest threat to sanity. In solitude the mind's initial "vacuity" asserted itself. Not filling itself with the objective contents of moral and intellectual experience which contact with other minds provided, it turned to Imagination for its food. Idle solitude implied

[1] By R. D. Havens, "Solitude and the Neoclassicists," *ELH*, XXI (1954), 251 f.
[2] *Correspondance Generale de J. J. Rousseau*, III, 370, quoted by Havens, "Solitude and the Neoclassicists," p. 267.

an escape from the world into a morass of subjectivity and amounted, therefore, to alienation from God and man. To detach oneself from moral concerns and social duties resulted in corruption and depravity, in a vacuity generating imagination to extremes of vice and madness. Solitude, reports Mrs. Thrale, in one of those quick paraphrases of hers, was described by Mr. Johnson as "dangerous even to the old and wise, how then shall the young resist its powerful Temptations? Life is a pill which cannot be swallowed without gilding, and if tumultuous Pleasures are refused us, we shall recur to those of mere Appetite; for the solicitations of Sense are always at hand. . . . The solitary mortal is certainly luxurious, probably superstitious and possibly mad: the mind stagnates for want of Employment; grows morbid, and is extinguished like a Candle in foul air." [3] In a letter to Boswell the same notion recurs: "The great direction which Burton has left to . . . disordered men is this, *Be not solitary; Be not idle:* which I would thus modify;—if you are idle, be not solitary; if you are solitary, be not idle." [4] Throughout Johnson's own writings solitude appears as the condition which encourages secret vice and loose imagination. The message of the Eighty-ninth *Rambler* is typical: some people who appear diligent and virtuous to the world may secretly "give themselves up to the luxury of fancy, please their minds with regulating the past, or planning the future . . . and slumber away their days in voluntary visions." [5]

When Johnson disapproved of this solitary dreamer who "retires to his apartments, shuts out the cares and interruptions of mankind, and abandons himself to his own fancy," he had, of course, himself in mind, for a brief glance at almost any passage in his diaries will show him repenting precisely such solitary and imaginative indolence. [6] But the moral message he was imparting was entirely conventional. Human imagination is a necessary concomitant of existence, and reason, as we shall see, is easily perverted, but one may remark in general that Johnson's concept of Imagination itself is rooted in a tradition of religious and moral thought that equated reason in its positive aspect with the divine and imagination in its negative aspect with the fallenness of man. It is therefore not surprising that the connection Johnson makes between solitude,

[3] *Thraliana*, I. 180.
[4] *Life*, III, 415.
[5] *Rambler* No. 89, *Works* II, 418-9.
[6] See, e.g., *Diaries*, pp. 50, 63, 64, 71, 73, 81-82.

sloth, imagination, and vice may be found in many literary antecedents and counterparts. As with so many of his ideas, Johnson was here depending on tradition no less than on his personal experience. Or perhaps one should say that his personal experience itself was always thought out in terms of the tradition.

Johnson's basic definition of the vacuity of the mind, his image of the mind as a vessel requiring to be "filled," and the idea that "the intellect . . . will embrace anything, however absurd or criminal, rather than be wholly without an object"— that vice "never takes such a firm possession of the mind as when it is found empty or unoccupied "[7]—is an axiom of Renaissance psychology, a rewording of ideas found in many writers. John Sym, for example, in his *Life's Preservative against Self Killing* (1637), remarks that "when the heart is not taken up with holy thoughts, and with good and warrantable employments in some calling, there is room, and fit time, for the *devill* to cast in his fiery temptations." [8]

The idea can in fact be traced to the earliest doctrines and institutions of Christianity. For example, "we charge you brethren . . . that you withdraw yourselves from every brother walking disorderly, and not according to the tradition received from us . . . for we were not disorderly among you. Neither did we eat any man's bread for nothing, but in labour and in toil we worked night and day" (II Thess. 3: 6–8). In writing this St. Paul was founding what was to be a long tradition of Christian diligence. By "disorderly persons" he meant people who broke the rules of the society in which God had placed them and who, thinking the impending End made their earthly obligations pointless, gave in to slothfulness and disorder. Paul calls upon them to live sanely, to await the Reversal of Nature "with quietness, to work and eat their own bread" (II Thess. 3:12). This aspect of Paul's practical teaching (see also I Thess. 4: 9–12; I Cor. 20 f) became central in the institution of monastic life, in which asceticism, contemplation, and prayer are reinforced by strict regularity and diligence. St. John Cassian (c.435) in his discussion of the eight chief hindrances to a monk's perfection had precisely this kind of neurotic idleness in mind when he spoke of the diabolical spirit of accidia, and his description brings Johnson's *Diaries* to mind. The spirit of accidia, Cassian writes, when it afflicts

---

[7] *Rambler* No. 85, *Works*, II, 402. This notion is also central in *Rasselas*.
[8] Sym, *Life's Preservative against Self Killing* (London, 1637), p. 217.

a man, "will not let him rest in his cell nor give himself to reading
. . . For every task to be done within the confines of his dwelling,
it makes him slow and indolent. . . . The fifth or sixth hour inflicts
him with weariness of body, and such appetite for food that he
seems as if he had just come from a long journey or was worn out
with terrific toil, or as if he had not taken food after two or three
days fast." [9]

Johnson's portrayal in the Eighty-ninth *Rambler* of the slothful
and sinful dreamer who retires from the world and abandons himself
to fancy, so that "new worlds rise up before him, one image is
followed by another, and a long succession of delights dances
around him," was, in fact, the conventional picture of the vice of
sloth, or accidia, which was traditionally seen as "charming down
the resistance" [10] of its victim by means of its siren song, casting a
diabolical spell over him, and offering to give his Imagination full
rein to wander through the most delightful (and sinful) scenes. An
interesting example of this can be found in Sir William Denny's
Pelicancidium; or the Christian Adviser against Self-Murder (1653), in
which the charms of indolence are portrayed as mysteriously evil and
decadent. The entire first canto of Book II in the *Pelicancidium* is
devoted to "the Den of Idleness," a dark cave in which the "Witch
of Idleness" lies sleeping. Around her stand her servants, the Vices,
and near the opening of her cave are scattered traps—"Dangers"
and "Delays"—covered with leaves. Near the cave's entrance there
is a spring of clear water. As the water returns to earth it gathers into
a stagnant pool, "a standing scum of stinking Drain" which
generates poisonous serpents and ugly toads. The way in which
slothful retirement from moral concerns frees and awakens the
dormant power of what in Johnson's version became the highly
generalized concept of Imagination is particularly emphasized in the
prose "Perspective" Denny supplies to clarify the moral of his
emblem. The den is

dark by ignorance. It is foul by sloth. Vices and sins, *like Monsters,
Exuberances of the Minde,* do breed therein, that hisse with Impudence, and
howl by too late Repentance. The hag, the Witch layes along, to shew her
Security and Carelessness, half asleep, her Improvidence, by stretching,

[9] *A Master of the Desert, Readings from John Cassian,* arr. and ed. W. B. Trevelyan
(London, 1927), pp. 83–85.
[10] *Works,* II, 419.

Indisposition to Imployment, and by scowling Scorn at Reproof. . . *Vain Discourses and wanton Designs are the Spring at the mouth of her Den*, which dance to the Notes of the Birds of Pleasure.[11]

The same traditional allegory, in Johnson's century, appears in James Thomson's *Castle of Indolence* (1748). Like Denny's "Den of Indolence" in the *Pelicancidium*, inhabited by a drowsy[12] witch, Thomson's castle belongs to a wizard who tempts people with the enchantments of euphoria and narcotic dreams of joy. Thomson first points out (in exquisite pseudo-Spenserian stanzas) that man must not complain about the "sad sentence of an ancient date" under which he is fated to spend his present life in toil, because

Without ten that would come an heavier bale,
Loose life, unruly passions, and diseases pale

(and this one of Johnson's favorite themes.) Similar to Denny's witch in her lowly situated cave, surrounded by shadows, luxuriance, and the atmosphere of stagnation, Thomson's wizard has constructed his castle in "lowly dale, fast by a river's side,"[13] and into it he entices weary pilgrams who wish to refresh themselves. Once in the castle, his victims sink into a torpor amid delightful sounds and sights. Thomson connects the pleasure of the free play of fancy with the sinful state of solitary sloth throughout the poem:

Nought but shadowy forms were seen to move,
As Idleness fancied in her dreamy mood.[14]

Johnson's solitary dreamer in *Rambler* No. 89, before whose eyes "new worlds live up" and "one image follows another" in "a long succession of delights," would be a typical visitor in the domain of

---

[11] *Pelicancidium; or the Christian Adviser against Self-Murder. Together with a Guide, and the Pilgrims Pass to the Land of the Living* (London, 1653), i, 36–38.

[12] "Immoderate sleep" in particular was sometimes connected in the Renaissance mind with the evil "imagination" of witchcraft. Platerus (Felix Plater), one of Burton's chief medical sources, describes in his section on the "consternation of the mind" the symptoms of the "preternatural sleep" which is the consequence of spiritual disturbance: "that is a *preternatural sleep* which lasts longer than a natural, and then it is called immoderate . . . sometimes also it invadeth with Ravings." Platerus goes on to discuss at great length the causes, symptoms, and cure of "immoderate sleep," "profound sleep," "Lethargie," "Sleep with Deliration," and "Diabolical Sleep." Platerus, *A Golden Practice of Physick, Unto Which is added two excellent Treatises. I. Of the French Pox, II. of the Gout* (London, 1662), p. 4 f.

[13] *Castle of Indolence*, I, 2, in *Thomson's Works*, ed. J. L. Robertson (Oxford, 1908), p. 253 f.

[14] *Ibid.*, I, 5.

Thomson's conventional "Wizard Indolence," the "pleasing land of drowsyhead," where "whatever smacked of noyance or unrest" was "far off expelled." [15]

In modern usage, when we speak of a conception as "purely imaginary," we mean on the whole that it does not correspond to the reality of things. "You are imagining things" means that these things are present only in your imagination, that they do not correspond to the objective state of affairs, although there is still a vestige of the old implication of hope and fear. In early usage, imagination was frequently more directly connected with evil, disorder, vanity, falsehood, and madness, as an examination of the adjectives that idiomatically went with it reveals. A "vain imagination," a "false imagination," and, in particular, a "mad imagination" were common phrases in everyday speech and were charged with connotations of total irrationality, sorcery, and irreligion. Imagination immediately implied madness. Abraham Fleming, for example, recounts how the Athenians "took Solon's true tale for a vaine toy . . . his undoubted divinations, *madde imaginations*." [16] Madness, in turn, was immediately associated with diabolical interference or possession. The devil himself was regarded as proverbially out of his wits; he was an "imaginative" creature. Further on in the *Panoplie*, Fleming tells of the Aberdites' judgment that Democritus, whose "*head was fraught with myllians of imaginations*, was "phrenetique and utterly dispossessed of reason . . . not maister of his own will . . . altogether ignorant whereabouts he was busied"—in short, "as mad as the devil in hell, or worse." [17] In Johnson's own century, Swift lists in the *Tale of a Tub* what he considers the mad philosophies of Epicurus, Descartes, and others under the category of "imaginations." [18] The association of Imagination and Pride is central to many of his writings, notably *Gulliver's Travels*.

The earliest known appearance of "vain imagination" directly connects it with sin and with the deceiving powers of the devil. Richard Rolle of Hampole in the early fourteenth century (in his *Psalter*, circa 1340), interpreted Psalm 37:7 thus "(Quoniam lumbi

---

[15] *Ibid.*, I, 6.
[16] Fleming, *A Panoplie of Epistles, Or, a looking Glass for the Unlearned* (London, 1576), p. 193.
[17] *Ibid.*, p. 277.
[18] "Digression Concerning Madness," *A Tale of a Tub*, Sec. IX, p. 107.

mei impleti sunt illusionibus: & non est sanitas in carne mea):
for my lendis ful ere fild of hethyngis: and hele is not in my fleysse.
My lendes, that is my fleysse, is fild of hethyngis of the devel, for
.i. syn not anly for my frelte, bot alswa of the fende, that
tournmentis my body and travails my saule in vayn ymaginations;
and swa makis he me his hethynge." [19] This was a primary sense of
the word until at least the seventeenth century. Burton was using the
word in Richard Rolle's sense when he remarked that men given to
"overmuch meditation" are open to *"the fears and imaginations"*
which attend upon Religious Despair.[20] Donne in his sermon on
Psalm 38:9 shows explicitly and eruditely how imagination and the
spontaneously sinful impulses and temptations of mankind are
connected: "all the imaginations of the thoughts of our hearts are
only evill continually; These imaginations, *ipsa figmenta*, as the
originall word *Jetzer* imports, before it come to be a formall and
debated thought . . . these imaginations and all these imaginations
they are evill." [21] It is in this sense—the sense of Richard Rolle,
Fleming, Burton, and Donne—that Johnson's notion of Imagination
becomes theologically significant. For it is in this sense that
imagination and retirement from ordinary human concerns imply
one another, the sense of Horatio's remark that Hamlet, who madly
insists on following the Ghost, "waxes desperate with
imagination." [22]

To say, therefore, that Johnson's concept of Imagination was
rooted in the medieval mentality which equated sin with diabolical
interference and mental disorder with possession by evil spirits is not
as paradoxical as may first appear. Johnson's axiomatic belief that
virtue necessarily implies commitment, in the sense of real moral
concern, and represents the regulation of the subjective Imagination
by means of objective Reason, is of course the mark of his humanism;
it is the basic assumption of Classical and Renaissance civilization,
and in a sense of the Middle Ages as well. But, in Johnson, the

[19] R. Rolle of Hampole, *The Psalter or Psalms of David and Certain Canticles*, ed.,
H. R. Bromley (Oxford, 1884), p. 139.
[20] *Anatomy of Melancholy*, 3: 4: 2: 3.
[21] *The Sermons of John Donne*, ed., G. R. Potter and M. Simpson (10 vols.;
Berkeley and Los Angeles, 1955), II, Sermon No. 6, p. 153. Donne is referring to
Genesis 6:5 "Yetzer machshevot libo rak ra kol hayom," which is rendered in the
Authorized Version as "every imagination of the thoughts of his heart was only evil
continually."
[22] *Hamlet*, I. iv. 87.

humanistic aspect is subtly blended with the Christian-medieval. The way in which he treats the psychological dangers of solitude and sloth (which in the old sin-lists meant a lack of spiritual zeal or a profound refusal of all spiritual effort rather than mere laziness) retains a strongly medieval flavor. The visions of Johnson's solitary dreamer in the Eighty-ninth *Rambler* are of the same order as Spenser's "Bower of Bliss" or Faustus' vision of Helen, and Johnson's concept of Imagination is a late metamorphosis of what medieval man regarded literally as the mysterious workings of the devil in the soul of a man guilty of that *evagatio mentis circa illicita*[23] which slothful solitude inevitably entailed.

Most of Johnson's remarks on solitude connect it with a subjectivism and self-centeredness which is condemned by means of the usual Christian-Humanist insistence that man was born to live in society and that virtue therefore cannot be achieved outside it. On this level idle solitude implies the refusal of effort and the lack of social involvement which can only lead to a complete distortion of values. It is a spiritual isolation from mankind, like that of the Old Man in Chapter XLV of *Rasselas*, who "cannot extend his interest beyond himself." The association of solitude with idleness runs through most of what Johnson said and wrote on the subject. Writing to Mrs. Thrale, he says, "company is in itself better than solitude, and pleasure better than indolence." [24] By saying "in itself" Johnson indicates that he is thinking in generic terms: company is generally better than isolation for the simple reason that isolation implies for him inaction. The sloth which in *The Vanity of Human Wishes* is described as a sin that "effuse[s] her opiate fumes" (l. 150) is the first step toward imaginative wish fulfillment and ultimate madness. "Solitude (added he one day) is dangerous to reason, without being favourable to virtue." [25]

I have already referred to the letter in which Johnson commented on Burton's "great direction." The connection Johnson

[23] St. Gregory, *Moralia in Job*, XXXI, xiv, quoted in P. Alphandèry, "De quelques documents medievaux relatifs a des états psychoastheniques," *Journal de Psychologie*, XXVI, 767–8. The opinions of the Fathers in this matter are summed up briefly under "Accidia" in the *Dictionary of the Apostolic Church*, ed. J. Hastings (Edinburgh, 1915). A more comprehensive summary is given in the *Dictionnaire de Spiritualité*, ed. M. Viller (Paris, 1938) and in M. W. Bloomfield, *The Seven Deadly Sins* (Michigan, 1952).

[24] *Life*, I, 145 n.

[25] *J.M.*, I, 219.

makes between idleness and solitude is indeed the connection Burton makes in the *Anatomy of Melancholy*, which ends with the injunction to "take this for a Corellary and conclusion as thou tenderest thine good, in this [religious melancholy] and in all other melancholy, thy good health of body and minde, observe this short precept, give not way to solitariness and idlenesse. *Be not alone, be not idle*." [26] Throughout the book Burton frequently repeats his advice to physicians to see that religious melancholics and persons suffering from despair of salvation should "not bee left solitary, or to themselves, never idle, never out of company." [27] Johnson's conviction that " solitude is a state dangerous to those accustomed to sink into themselves," [28] that "melancholy shrinks from communication," [29] and that solitary self-indulgence or luxury "lets in disease to seize upon her worshipers" [30] owes much to Burton. The *Anatomie of Melancholy*, Johnson said, was the only book "that ever took him out of bed two hours sooner than he wished to rise." [31] He mentioned the book in conversation frequently[32] and gave it to Mrs. Thrale to read.[33] He always seems to have considered Burton the most relevant among the many writers he had consulted on the subject of mental disorder, as well as a forceful literary artist.

Johnson's predominant idea of solitude comes out when he notes that the intolerable boredom produced by solitary inactivity may well lead to drink ("a dram to a vacant and solitary person is speedy and seducing relief") [34] and that a man's imagination is freer to range when he is alone than when he is restricted by social intercourse. All temptations are greater in the solitary state. As he put it in the eighth *Rambler*, we "may corrupt our hearts in the most recluse solitude, with more pernicious and tyrannical appetites and wishes than the commerce of the world will generally produce." [35]

[26] *Anatomy of Melancholy*, 3:4:2:6.
[27] *Ibid.*, 3:4:2:2.
[28] *Rambler* No. 89, *Works*, II, 419.
[29] *Rasselas*, chap. xlvii.
[30] *Rambler* No. 33, *Works*, II, 164.
[31] *Life*, II, 121.
[32] See e.g., *Life*, II, 121, 446; III, 415; V, 554.
[33] *Thraliana*, I, 536–7.
[34] *J.M.*, I, 219.
[35] *Works*, II, 37.

But in the case of solitude, as in most other matters, Johnson tries to see both sides. In many of the writings he notes the *uses*, the moral and religious utility, of a certain kind of solitude. In two essays, the Seventh *Rambler* and *Adventurer* No. 126, he elaborately argues the religious uses of a periodic retirement from the world, and it is in these essays that we see the basis of his ambivalent attitude toward monasticism. Such retirement is of course something quite different from the romantic solitude advocated by Rousseau (in the *Rêveries du Promeneur Solitaire*, for example). In fact, it is its diametrical opposite. In the *Adventurer* No. 126, Johnson comments on the fashionable praise of solitude and immediately goes on to tie it with imagination and hope. (This in itself should be sufficient proof of Johnson's authorship of this paper.)[36] "Almost every man delights his imagination with the hopes of obtaining some time an opportunity of retreat." For the most part, however, those who cherish the dream of solitude are motivated by pure egocentricity: they "have no higher or remoter view, than the present gratification of their passions." What they are really after is a life in "perpetual compliance with their own inclinations, without the necessity of regulating their actions by any other man's convenience or opinion." These are the men who find virtue simply too difficult—the self-indulgent, who cannot really "regulate" their lives. Others, "more delicate and tender," are offended by the vices and defects of society and believe that flight from social ills will provide them with tranquility. But both the egocentrics and the escapists will be disappointed in their expectations of solitary contentment. The former will find that they are social creatures after all, if only in that their high opinion of themselves depends on the flattery of others, whereas the latter, "whose faculties are employed in too close an observation of failings and defects, will find [their] condition very little mended by transferring [their] attention from others to [themselves"][37]

The general drift of the argument thus depends on the crucial difference Johnson sees between, on the one hand, the universal *dream* of solitude, the hope or expectation that retirement from society will bring happiness, and, on the other, the *reality* of solitude,

---

[36] For an authentication of Johnson's authorship, see L. F. Powell, "Johnson's Part in *The Adventurer*," *RES*, III (1927), 420–29.

[37] *Works*, IV, 125.

with its tendency to promote subjectivity and therefore madness. It is this discrepancy between the imaginative desire and its fulfillment in reality that makes the dream of solitude as vain as all other imaginative human wishes, and it is exposed in *Rasselas*, like the rest, when Nekayah absurdly dreams of her pastoral retreat.

But in the *Adventurer* No. 126 one kind of solitude remains that does not completely fall in this category. In his attitude toward monastic life Johnson condemns the solitary idleness asceticism produces at its worst but takes into account the beneficial "regulation of life" it imposes at its best. To Mrs. Thrale he remarked that "convents are *idle* places" and that "the insipidity of Monastic life" could easily "produce madness." [38] But in *Rasselas* the monks of St. Anthony are praised for leading a strictly regulated life, devoted exclusively to labor and meditation. Whatever they do, we are told, can be said to have been "incited by an adequate and reasonable motive," because "their time is regularly distributed; one duty succeeds another so that they are not . . . lost in the shades of listless inactivity." [39] His reverence for the self-abnegation of monastic life is reflected in the tendency of his entire moral system toward that *other* state of being—the state of pure piety and contemplation in which the soul is released from vacuity, imagination, hope, and habit. "I never read of a hermit," he confesses, "but in imagination I kiss his feet; never of a monastery but could fall down on my knees and kiss the pavement." [40] These are the sentiments underlying the conclusion of *Adventurer* No. 126, in which we are told that the *intention* of religious recluses "entitles them to a higher respect" than those who quit the world for worldly reasons, that although the highest order of men "are placed in an evil world, to exhibit public examples of good life," we must "look with veneration" also upon those who, not being able to resist the temptations ever-present in communal life, retire from society to achieve sanctity in solitude.

The conclusion of the thirty-second *Idler*, an essay devoted to the subject of sleep, embodies what is perhaps Johnson's most complete and concentrated statement on solitude; a statement that gains full meaning only when we are familiar with Johnson's central

[38] *Thraliana*, I, 183.
[39] *Rasselas*, chap. xlvii.
[40] *Life*, V, 62.

concept of the disorderly Imagination which evades reality and the "regulated" Reason which confronts it. Solitude, we are told, is for many people an opportunity to unbridle their Imagination, "which sometimes puts sceptres in their hands or mitres on their heads, shifts the scene of pleasure with endless variety . . . and gluts them with every change of visionary luxury." In other words, solitude is sought by wordly men because in the social state the ambitious mind is frustrated by realities alien to its basic need for *absolute* satisfaction. In social life "endless variety" is a contradiction in terms, since all variety becomes monotony in time and no "glutting" is possible because all temporal satisfactions are surpassed by the mind's extratemporal need. Such solitude, then, is at root both an attempt to escape from the boredom inherent in temporal existence and an attempt to escape from the limitations of present realities. In the "semi-slumbers" of solitude, Imagination is given full rein to "bring back the past . . . anticipate the future . . . and forget that misery is the lot of man." The "semi-slumbers" of solitude are "a voluntary dream, a temporary recession from the realities of life to airy fictions—and *habitual subjection of reason to fancy.*"

In the concluding paragraph of this *Idler* we get the real meaning of solitude, as opposed to the escapist dream of retirement. In reality, human solitude is far more than the literal absence of other persons. One might go so far as to say that here solitude is seen as an inevitable condition of the soul, since Johnson fully recognizes the solitude of man even while in the company of his fellows. Or rather, man avoids his fellows and seeks their company for a similar reason, a reason rooted in the core of his misery and of his need to escape harsh reality: "Others are afraid to be alone, and amuse themselves by a perpetual succession of companions; but the difference is not great; in solitude we have our dreams to ourselves, and in company we agree to dream in concert. The end sought in both is forgetfulness of ourselves." This is perhaps the epitome of Johnson's pessimism, the sad truth underlying the gay assemblies of Cairo, among whom, Imlac says, "there was not one who did not dread the moment when solitude should deliver him to the tyranny of reflexion." [41]

[41] *Rasselas*, chap. xvi.

By referring the self-indulgence implicit in the romantic dream of solitude to the unbearable reality of solitude as a self-confrontation, Johnson thus returns to his central theme: the essential inadequacy of human life on earth. The need for solitude is shown as an escapist dream, an impossibility, a manifestation of the mind's inherent and futile craving for absolute fulfillment, a possibility for relative sanctity; and at the same time as the very core of the human situation.

CHAPTER FIVE: THE GENERAL AND PARTICULAR

*I*mlac's dictum that *"the business of a poet is to examine, not the individual, but the species"* [1] *has been studied in the light of Johnson's other statements on the relative importance of particularity and generality in poetry and has been convincingly related to the eighteenth-century concern with the "sublime"* [2] *but it has not, so far as I know, been considered in relation to what is perhaps more fundamental for an understanding of Johnson's aesthetics: the moral and religious observations which form the core of his thought.* Since for Johnson, as for many other eighteenth-century writers, the religious, the moral, and the aesthetic were not, what they later became, separate spheres (Imlac "the poet" is in fact the moral sage in *Rasselas*), it seems to me that his views on the nature and function of poetry are best understood in terms of his more general ideas concerning the nature of man. In the present chapter I propose to follow Johnson's dictum and to attempt a wider examination of generality and particularity as key notions not merely in his theory of poetry but also in the body of thought which emerges from a reading of all his principal religious and moral writings.

[1] *Rasselas*, chap. x, p. 62.

[2] By Scott Elledge, "The Background and Development in English Criticism of the Theories of Generality and Particularity," *PMLA*, LXII (1947), 147–82. See also S. H. Monk, *The Sublime: A Study of Critical Theories in XVIII Century England* (New York, 1935); W. K. Wimsatt, Jr., " The Structure of the Concrete Universal in Literature," *PMLA*, LXII (1947), 262–80; W. K. Wimsatt, Jr., and C. Brooks, *Literary Criticism: A Short History* (New York, 1957), chap. xv; R. McKeon, "Literary Criticism and the Concept of Imitation in Antiquity," *Modern Philology*, XXXIV (1936), 1–35; and L. I. Bredvold, "The Tendency Toward Platonism in Neo-Classical Esthetics," *ELH*, I (1934), 91–119. The issue of generality versus particularity in Johnson's criticism is discussed by W. J. Bate in his *From Classic to Romantic* (New York, 1946), chap. 3, but his conclusions are disowned or at least corrected in his later study, *The Achievement of Samuel Johnson* (New York, 1961), pp. 198–200. In J. H. Hagstrum's discussion of the topic, Johnson's empirical, Lockian element is stressed; see *Samuel Johnson's Literary Criticism* (Minneapolis, 1952), chap. 1.

Perhaps the first thing to notice concerning the role of
generality and particularity in Johnson's view of man is the idea
that, although the will, and consequently "the attention" of men as
we observe them existing in time, fixes upon *particular* objects,
man's real being, unlike that of beasts, is essentially defined by the
contradiction between a transcendence of and its employments in
time. The human will is seen as infinite and "general" in the sense
that it is a priori undifferentiated and objectless.[3] The difference
between man and beast lies in the fact that animal desire has no
margins beyond its temporality. Animal desire does not need to
"fix" upon a particular object because it is by nature wholly oriented
toward specific temporal goals, whereas man's real craving transcends
nature. Man's earthly, temporal strivings are really expressions of a
hunger that is entirely beyond time:

> "What" said [Rasselas], "makes the difference between man and all the
> rest of the animal creation? Every beast that strays beside me has the same
> corporeal necessities with myself: he is hungry and crops the grass, he is
> thirsty and drinks the stream; his thirst and hunger are appeased, he is
> satisfied and sleeps . . . I am hungry and thirsty like him, but when thirst
> and hunger cease I am not at rest; *I am like him pained with want, but am not*
> *like him satisfied with fulness.*"[4]

Man, unlike the beasts, is restless and "uneasy"[5] in a world of
fluctuation and differentiation. His restlessness, which springs from
the unalterable contradiction between his metaphysical,
undifferentiated desire and its differentiated mock fulfillments in
time, makes him concentrate all his powers upon *particular* temporal
ends which he imaginatively elevates to that dignity of absolute
value which only the truly general and unspecified can have. Such
transformation may be objectively absurd, but, when seen from
within the human condition, must be recognized as the essence of
temporal life. A lack of particular desire is a "vacuity," a condition
of "tediousness" or "torpidity"[6] that may culminate in madness
(since the mind will invent particular ends-of-desire that have no
relation to reality and will shape itself accordingly). Consciousness

---

[3] See Chapter 1, "The Vacuity of Life."

[4] *Rasselas*, chap. ii, p. 41.

[5] Cf., *Life*, II, 73: "As to care or mental uneasiness [savages] are not above it, but
below it, like bears."

[6] Cf., e.g., *Rasselas*, chap. xi, p. 66: "Ignorance . . . is a vacuity in which the soul
sits motionless and torpid for want of attraction."

must have particular objects to attend to in the real world; the extratemporal will must fasten upon particular temporal goals or be utterly frustrated by inaction, by a negation of what the process of time itself dictates. "If I had any known want," says Rasselas, "I should have *a certain wish:* that wish would excite endeavour and I should not then repine to see the sun move so slowly . . . I fancy that I should be happy if I had *something* to pursue." [7] The "hunger of imagination which preys upon life" must be "appeased by *some* employment." [8]

The mind's attempts to find proper objects within time thus lead it to narrow the general will which is its supratemporal nature and to ascribe value to the particular. Man "devotes his heart"[9] to definite objects of pursuit and his attention becomes "fixed upon" [10] narrow, differentiated goals. But this concentration of human attention (I employ this word because it is so recurrent in Johnson's writings) upon a particular end can be possible only at the expense of attention to other particulars. The very act of ascribing (earthly) value to one thing involves the act of ignoring the possibility of value or interest in other things. Johnson therefore sees, in the concern with particular ends which is so necessary a concomitant of temporal life, a symptom of man's irrationality, of what in the Johnsonian ethos is designated as Imagination. It is Imagination that concentrates upon some particular to the exclusion of others, in the same sense that Reason surveys particulars in the context of a whole. Reason leads to truth, Imagination to error and delusion. But Imagination is, as I have noted, inextricably woven into human life and consciousness; the process of life from moment to moment enables particular objects to conquer our attention by arousing our hopes or fears. That our concentration upon one thing makes us blind to others is thus the essence of human limitation. No man can be (or should expect to be) purely rational. Imlac himself, recounting his life to the prince, tells how "when *this thought* [of the imagined happiness that awaited him in his native land] had *taken*

---

[7] *Rasselas*, chap. iii, p. 44.
[8] *Ibid.*, chap. xxxii, p. 113.
[9] *Rambler* No. 58, *Works*, II, 277.
[10] Nekayah, perceiving her brother's "attention fixed, proceeded in her narrative" (*Rasselas*, chap. xxvi, p. 96). "Curiosity . . . *fixes the attention*" (*Idler* No. 57, *Works*, IV, 317).

possession of my mind, I considered every moment as wasted that did not bring me nearer to Abyssinia."[11]

Reason and Imagination form the basic polarity of concepts that underlies all of Johnson's generalizations about man. Imagination is the faculty which leads the mind into error by distorting, limiting, or hiding the true state of affairs in accordance with the heart's perverse desires and needs. Reason, on the other hand, is that which discloses the true state of affairs and which thus controls (or "regulates," as Johnson frequently puts it) the impulses of Imagination. If the notion of Imagination may be associated with the limited viewpoint, with passion, with a projection of value upon *particular* ends (and with subjection to time), Reason is linked with the *general* viewpoint, with the evaluation of particular objects in terms of a larger context, and with that which is not dependent upon or subject to time. Inasmuch as man is inescapably a creature of Imagination as well as a rational being, his limited awareness inevitably entails basic error. Since no man can "take in the whole concatenation of causes and effects . . . where . . . is the wonder that they who see only a small part should judge erroneously of the whole?" [12]

The theme of the limitation of human attention and awareness to selected particulars recurs throughout Johnson's writings and conversation. Nekayah, in the "Debate on Marriage," suggests that people do not act "with *all* the reasons of action present to their minds" and that this fact points to what is "the state of mankind." [13] In *Rambler* No. 203 we learn that "the eye of the mind, like that of the body, can only extend its view to new objects, by losing sight of those which are now before it" [14]—a statement pointing to the connection I have already indicated between the temporal nature of human awareness and its limiting confinement to particulars. In *Rambler* No. 108 we are told that "of extensive surfaces we can only take a survey, as the parts succeed one another." [15] During a discussion of Hume, Johnson remarked that "the human mind is so limited that it cannot take in all the parts of a subject, so that there

---

[11] *Rasselas,* chap. xii, p. 58. Cf., chap. xlvii, p. 150: the Astronomer's "reason had been . . . *subjugated by an uncontrollable and overwhelming idea."*

[12] *Adventurer* No. 107, *Works,* IV, 95.

[13] *Rasselas,* chap. xxix, p. 106.

[14] *Works,* III, 443.

[15] *Ibid.,* 12.

may be objections raised against anything," [16] and in the *Adventurer* No. 107—a paper which contains what is perhaps the most complete discussion of the subject—we learn that "disagreement of opinion . . . will be multiplied . . . *because we are finite beings*, furnished with different *degrees of attention*, and discovering consequences which escape another, none taking in the whole concatenation of causes and effects, and most comprehending but *a very small part.*" [17] The religious basis of this recurrent insistence on human limitation to particularity as a symptom of man's creatureliness and irrationality is made quite clear in this essay: "life is not the object of science; *we see a little, a very little . . . .* the only thought, therefore, on which we can repose with comfort, is that which presents us to the care of *Providence, whose eye takes in the whole of things.*" [18]

The butt of Augustan satire is frequently the man of "useless" learning who has concentrated all his attention upon single aspects of experience at the expense of all others. He is the man who does not see his own pursuit as a detail in a more general picture of human life to which it is and must be subservient. The exclusive concern of Swift's Laputans with mathematics, astronomy, and music, for example, points to their total irrationality. They represent in unadulterated form what Johnson (and many before him, including Swift himself)[19] designated as Imagination. Their mad obsession with the abstract disciplines makes them lose sight of the "usefulness" that characterizes true rationality and which can be achieved only by a balancing view of one's particular pursuit within the perspective of the whole. Their total inability to see things in context points to their essential guilt of pride, of concentration upon self, of what Swift saw as the profoundest kind of impiety and irrationality (for the two ultimately come to the same thing). Again, in the Fourth Book of the *Dunciad* there is an amusing episode in which the Goddess of Dulness is called upon to settle a quarrel

[16] *Life*, I, 444.

[17] *Works*, IV, 95; cf., *Idler* No. 5, *ibid.*, 163, "of all extensive and complicated objects, different parts are selected by different eyes; and minds are variously affected as they *vary their attention.*"

[18] *Works*, IV, 99. Cf., Pope's insistence in the *Essay on Man* that "Tis but a part we see and not a whole" (Epistle I, l. 60), whereas "the first Almighty Cause/Acts not by partial, but by gen'ral laws" (ll. 145–46). "Each individual seeks a sev'ral goal;/But HEAVENS great view is One, and that the Whole" (Epistle II, ll. 237–38).

[19] See, e.g., *Tale of a Tub*, Sec. IX, where "imagination" is used as an interchangeable term for "cant," "vision," and "deception."

between two natural scientists. The plaintiff tells how he had reared a flower that was the most beautiful ever seen; he had devoted his entire life to the delightful plant, had spread its leaves "soft on paper ruffs," and had lovingly named it "Caroline." Then, he weepingly complains, an insensitive ruffian trampled the flower into the dust. But the accused has an analogous story with which to justify himself. He had seen a lovely butterfly which he pursued until it had landed on the flower. When he pounced to seize it, he had indeed destroyed the flower, but, says this entomologist,

> Rose or Carnation was below my care;
> I meddle, Goddess! only in my sphere.[20]

The Goddess settles the dispute by blessing both dunces and exclaims:

> O! would the Sons of Men once think their Eyes
> And Reason given them but to study Flies!
> See Nature in some partial, narrow shape,
> And let the Author of the whole escape.[21]

The portrayal of dunce scientists, of pedants, virtuosi, enthusiasts, and projectors in eighteenth-century satire is intended to expose the roots of human discord, faction, and erroneous opinion. Underlying these grotesqueries is the assumption that were men more rational no disagreement or clash would occur. Satires like the Tale of a Tub, Gulliver's Travels, and the Dunciad deal basically with what their authors saw as the profound irrationality of man, an irrationality manifested in the limited view which so concentrates upon particulars as to completely lose sight of the general. The whole, the general, grasped by pious reason—as is made so vivid in Windsor Forest and the Essay on Man—is in turn identified with beauty, harmony, usefulness, and agreement of details.

This association of unreason with the particular and of reason with the general is a cornerstone of Johnson's thought on many subjects. The concentration upon certain aspects of experience at the expense of others, which, as we have seen, is inevitable in finite existence, explains the inability of men to communicate rationally with one another; it explains the proliferation of contradictory

---

[20] Dunciad, Book IV, ll. 431–33.
[21] Ibid., 453–56. Cf., the satirical portrait of Quisquilius, the virtuoso-collector, in Rambler No. 82, and the analysis in Rambler No. 83.

opinions in almost any matter; and by extension it underlies the entire social fabric of man.

> Whatever has various respects, must have various appearances of good and evil, beauty and deformity; thus, the gardener tears up as a weed the plant which the physitian gathers as a medicine; and "a general," says Sir Kenelm Digby, "will look with pleasure over a plain, as a fit place on which the fate of empires might be decided in battle, which the farmer will despise as bleak and barren, neither fruitful of pasturage, nor fit for tillage . . ." Two men examining the same question proceed commonly like the physitian and gardener in selecting herbs or the farmer and hero looking on the plain; *they bring minds impressed with different notions, and direct their inquiries to different ends;* they form, therefore, contrary conclusions and each wonderes at the other's absurdity.[22]

In the *Adventurer* No. 128, Johnson writes that to a man of one profession men of another may appear absurd precisely because what seems to one of absolute value does not interest others. The crucial notion is again the notion of "attention"; we do not ascribe value to what has not caught our attention. What does not interest us can have no significance for us. We believe that we regard some particular interest, which we do not share, with a kind of objectivity, for we are outside the consciousness which has given it value, but ultimately one man's view of another's pursuit or calling is not really detached, since it is determined and limited by his own interests. If he finds the partiality of others absurd, this may be ascribed to the fact that "by a partial and imperfect representation, may everything be made equally ridiculous." [23]

The entire analysis depends on Johnson's primary concern with the effects of time. Our particular preoccupations are "radicated by time." Those limited objects of life which have interested us over a long period determine our individuality, our nature. Habit confirms our partial evaluations in our minds. It places us with increasing firmness within a given role that is determined by those things which have "gained our attention." Time itself has the effect of making men's basic attitudes more insular. They become increasingly incapable of taking the general view which would place all particulars, including the objects of their own hopes and fears,

[22] *Adventurer* No. 107, *Works* IV, 95–6.
[23] *Works*, IV, 131.

within the context of a wider reality.[24] Thus, in the Fifty-sixth *Idler*, we learn that "there is such difference between the pursuits of men, that one part of the inhabitants of a great city lives to little other purpose than to wonder at the rest. *Some have hopes and fears, wishes and aversions, which never enter into the thoughts of others.*"[25] And in the the Sixtieth *Rambler:* "The man whose *faculties have been engrossed* by business, and whose heart never fluttered but at the rise and fall of the stocks, wonders how *the attention can be seized*, or the *affection agitated*, by a tale of love."[26] Imlac's father, who "desired only to be rich" could envisage no other pursuit worthy of his son,[27] and Imlac's own thirst for knowledge is equally described as a "predominant desire."[28]

Johnson's thought in this as in most matters is nourished by traditional ideas. Pekuah, who finds that the Arabs' *"predominant passion* was desire for money" echoes the traditional psychology which is the keynote of the Second Epistle of Pope's *Essay on Man:*

> As Man, perhaps, the moment of his breath,
> Receives the lurking principle of death,
> The young disease that must subdue at length,
> Grows with his growth, and strengthens with his strength:
> So, cast and mingled with his very frame,
> The Mind's disease, its RULING PASSION came,
> Each vital humour which should feed the whole,
> Soon flows to this, in body and in soul:
> Whatever warms the heart, or fills the head
> As the mind opens and its functions spread.
> Imagination plies her dangerous art,
> And pours it all upon the peccant part
> Nature its mother, Habit is its nurse;
> Wit, Spirit, Faculties, but make it worse;
> Reason itself but gives it edge and power;

---

[24] E.g., *Rasselas*, chap. xxix, p. 106: " . . . time itself, as it modifies unchangeably the external mien, determines likewise the direction of the passions." In the *Adventurer* No. 107 there is a metaphorical description of life which perfectly sums up the relation between the limits of attention and the effects of time: "At our first sally into the intellectual world, we all march together along one straight and open road; but *as we proceed further, and wider prospects open to our view, every eye fixes upon a different scene*, we divide into various paths, and, as we move forward, are still at a greater distance from each other" (*Works, IV*, 95).
[25] *Ibid.*, 315. Cf., *Rambler* No. 99, *ibid.*, II, 471: "the sailor, the academick, the lawyer, the mechanick, and the courtier, have all a cast of talk peculiar to their fraternity; have *fixed their attention* upon the same events."
[26] *Ibid.*, II, 286.
[27] *Rasselas*, chap. viii, p. 55.
[28] *Ibid.*, p. 57.

As Heaven's blest beam turns vinegar more sour . . .
Yes, Nature's road must ever be preferred;
Reason is here no guide, but still a guard:
'Tis hers to rectify, not overthrow,
And treat this passion more as friend than foe:
A mightier Power the strong direction sends,
And several Men impels to several ends . . .   (*II, 33–148, 161–67*)

But it is important to note that Johnson took strong exception to Pope's version of the theory, especially to what he saw as its tendency "to produce the belief of a kind of moral predestination, or overruling principle which cannot be resisted." In the *Life of Pope* he condemns Pope's "favourite theory of a Ruling Passion" (as set forth in the *Characters of Men*, 1734) for being "pernicious as well as false." The main difference between the versions of Pope and Johnson lies in the fact that for Pope the direction of the passions is potentially fixed "at the moment of breath," determining the nature of a man's whole life, whereas Johnson, insisting as always on the primacy of experience, on moral freedom and the necessity of choice, points out that "human characters are by no means constant . . . he who is at one time a lover of pleasure, is at another a lover of money." He further maintains that, inasmuch as men's lives do exhibit constant tendencies, their predominant orientation is fixed not by a pre-experiential determinism but by something that has early caught their *attention*—"not by an ascendant planet or predominating humor, but by the first book which they read, some early conversation which they heard, or some accident which excited ardour and emulation."[29] This is Johnson's point in *Rambler* No. 103, when he speaks of "the modern dream of a ruling passion," [30] and in *A View of the Controversy between Mons. Crousaz and Mr. Warburton on the Subject of Mr. Pope's Essay on Man;* it underlies his approval ("an observation which every writer ought to impress upon his mind") of Crousaz's assertion that "nothing so much hinders men from obtaining a complete victory over their ruling passion, as . . . a free intercourse . . . with libertines."[31]

Predominant desires fixing upon particular earthly events, the fact that "a lover finds no inclination to travel any path but that which leads to the habitation of his mistress [and] a trader can spare

[29] *Life of Pope*, in *Lives*, II, 279–80.
[30] *Works*, II, 489.
[31] Letter to the *Gentleman's Magazine*, XIII (1743), in *Works*, V, 203.

little attention to common occurrences, when his fortune is endangered by a storm,"[32] are, as we have seen, produced by Imagination, the fundamental characteristic of fallen man; but they are also necessarily at the root of civilized life and have their value in guarantying the integrity of the social structure. In fact, without the partiality of men for their own pursuits, no progress in these pursuits would be possible: "It may be observed in general, that no trade had ever reached the excellence to which it is now improved, had its professors looked upon it with the eyes of indifferent spectators, the advances, from the first rude essays, must have been made by men who valued themselves for performances, for which scarce any other would be persuaded to esteem them.[33]

Where, then, does imaginative partiality for one's pursuit cease to be subjective pride and become social virtue? At what point does involvement in one's particular end cease to be folly and become rational commitment to the realities of organized social life? The criterion, which Johnson shares with Pope, Swift, and their many humanist predecessors, is that of "use," the *utile*, which means the same thing when applied to social morality as it does when applied to art. Pope's botanist and entomologist need not have given up their particular interest in plants and butterflies to lose the status of dunces and gain that of humanists; their guilt and their absurdity lie in their having made their narrow interest so ruling a passion as to lose sight of all else, to lose sight of the "usefulness" which could have been a real moral justification for their particular passions: "This passion . . . like that for the grandeur of our own country, is to be *regulated*, not extinguished. Every man, from the highest to the lowest station, ought to warm his heart, and animate his endeavours with the hopes of being useful to the world, by advancing the art which it is his lot to exercise, and for that end he must necessarily consider the *whole extent* of its application, and the whole weight of its importance."[34]

Johnson's employment of the word "hopes" in this context is telling. For indeed what he is saying here about professional pride he would apply to all the earthly hopes which center in particular goals.

---

[32] *Rambler* No. 103, *Works*, II, 488.
[33] *Rambler* No. 9, *Works*, II, 42.
[34] *Ibid.*, p. 43. Cf., *Rambler* No. 99, *ibid.*, II, 471: "partiality is not wholly to be avoided, nor is it culpable, unless suffered so far *to predominate* as to produce aversion from every other kind of excellence."

Such hope is a necessary condition of human existence, its absence being the greatest of threats to sanity, but it can be prevented from turning itself into a mad and sinful obsession with particular ends only by the perspectives of rational judgment, by the balancing general view which provides an evaluation of the real "use" of that particular. The same commonsensical balancing of particular and general, or rather the same ascription of real value to the particular only inasmuch as it is subservient and "useful" to the general, lies at the core of Johnson's aesthetics.

The main use of poetry, according to Johnson, is as an antidote to Imagination. It must lead us toward whatever sanity we are capable of, protect us from the mad obsessions of the heart, and it can do this only by presenting us with the "stability of truth." By presenting truth it releases our "attention" and widens "the extent" of our views. When in Johnson's Christian imitation of Juvenal's Tenth Satire, we are invited to

> Let *observation* with extensive view,
> *Survey mankind, from China to Peru,*[35]

a rationality is invoked which would free us from our constricting private concerns by calling our attention to the general state of man. We are invited to widen our horizon in a way which should enable us to place each particular detail in the context of a whole, to notice what all may agree upon, for "we differ . . . when we see *only part* of the question . . . but when we perceive *the whole at once* . . . all agree in one judgement." [36] The same is true of *Rasselas*. In *The Vanity of Human Wishes*, the phrase "extensive view" becomes truly pregnant with meaning only when we appreciate the connotations it accrues by its connection with the Johnsonian view of the "limits" of human attention, for the imagery of mental width and narrowness recurs throughout his writings—width inevitably connected with Reason and narrowness allied to Imagination. "We grow more happy as our minds take a *wider range*," we are told in *Rasselas*.[37] Shakespeare's instructiveness is due to his *"wide extension of design."* [38] His "adherence to general nature has exposed him to the censure of

[35] *Vanity of Human Wishes*, ll. 1–2.
[36] *Rasselas*, chap. xxviii, p. 103.
[37] *Ibid.*, chap. xi, p. 66.
[38] *Preface to Shakespeare, Works*, V, 106.

critics, who form their judgements upon *narrower principles.*" [39]
Nekayah, investigating family life, meets the daughters of many
houses and finds "*their thoughts narrow*, their wishes low, and their
merriment often artificial," [40] while Pekuah tells how the Arab
women who were her sole companions in captivity could be neither
diverting nor instructive (the attributes of both art and rational
discourse) because "they had no ideas but of the few things that
were within their view." [41] The Prince's views, earlier in the book,
are described as "*extended to a wider space.*" [42]

In the poem, to observe with extensive view is to "remark *each*
anxious toil, *each* eager strife"; from the vantage point of rationality
to notice in proper context the *particular* manifestations of
imagination in many instances of men pursuing earthly goals; to
see how men become obsessed with "fancied ills" and "airy good,"
with the *imaginary* values of particular earthly ends; to observe
nations brought to ruin by "*darling* schemes," [43] i.e., by ideas of
worldly glory that become so obsessive as to exclude all rational
considerations. After noting how human "vent'rous pride" and
human imagination (concepts that are closely associated in Johnson's
mind since both lie at the core of human folly) are crushed by the
process of time that had brought them into being, we should find
ourselves in a position of truly rational, Christian pessimism. Having

[39] *Ibid.*, p. 109. Cf. Pope's remark in the *Essay on Criticism* (Epistle II, ll. 263–66)
that

> *Most Critics, fond of some subservient art*
> *Still make the whole depend upon the part*
> *They talk of principles, but notions prize,*
> *And all to loved folly sacrifice.*

Johnson thought very highly of the *Essay on Criticism*. See *Life of Pope*, in *Lives*, II,
229–30.

[40] *Rasselas*, chap. xxv, p. 95.

[41] *Ibid.*, chap. xxxix, p. 131.

[42] *Ibid.*, chap. iv, p. 45. Cf. also *Rambler* No. 80, *Works*, II, 375: "the hill flatters
with *an extensive view*"; *Rambler*, No. 78, *Works*, II, 367: "It is . . . the business of
wisdom and virtue, to select among numberless objects . . . such as may enable us
to *exalt our reason, extend our views, and secure our happiness*"; and *Rambler* No. 103,
Works, II, 488: "There are, indeed, beings in the form of men, who appear
satisfied with their intellectual possessions and seem to live without desire of
enlarging their conceptions."

[43] *Vanity of Human Wishes*, ll. 3–15. Cf. *Rambler* No. 56, *Works*, II, 269: "When
we see a man *pursuing some darling interest*, without much regard to the opinion of
the world, we justly consider him as corrupt and dangerous"; and *Rambler* No. 99,
Works, II, 471: "as limits must be always set to the excursions of the human mind,
there will be . . . *some darling subject* on which a man is principally pleased to
converse."

learned how vain are all temporal, particular pursuits, we must conclude that hope and fear can find their proper "objects" only outside time, in the *other* state of being taught by religion. The method of the poem remains continually that of the "extensive view." Whereas the narrow views which our obsessions impose upon us make us time's fools, because we are so immersed in ultimately absurd earthly hopes and fears, the wide perspective of the general human condition should lead us to a rational other-worldliness.[44] In quotidian life a "*particular* train of ideas *fixes the attention*," [45] a particular object "*intrenches itself* strongly in the mind" [46] or "*fastens upon*" it; [47] our thoughts may be "long fixed upon a single point," and consequently the "images of other things [will be] stealing away." [48] The deepest function of poetry is to dispel these fixations upon particular notions and to restore our sanity by calling our attention to the general truths about the condition of man which are the truths of religion.

Generality in art, then, signifies that which is common to all man, in all ages, "from China to Peru"; that which is essential in human nature. The particular in the aesthetic phase of Johnson's thought means the accidental and mutable. "Shakespeare always makes nature predominate over accident; and if he preserves *the essential character*, is not very careful of distinctions superinduced and adventitious. His story requires Romans and Kings, but he thinks only on men." [49] The true aim of art is precisely the aim of the moralist: to show "the uniformity in the state of man." A recognition of this basic uniformity is supremely important because by providing a release from the tensions of self and subjectivity it leads to salvation, and therefore we find it reiterated in varying contexts throughout Johnson's writings. In the Ninety-ninth *Adventurer*, we are told that "human nature is always the same." [50] In *Rasselas* we learn that the poet must trace "human nature through all its variations," [51] because fundamentally "nature and passion . . .

---

[44] See Chapter 7, "The Rationality of Faith."
[45] *Rasselas*, chap. xliv, p. 150.
[46] *Rambler* No. 58, *Works*, II, 277.
[47] *Rasselas*, chap. xlii, p. 137.
[48] *Ibid.*, chap. xl, p. 134.
[49] *Preface to Shakespeare*, *Works*, V, 109.
[50] *Works*, IV, 85.
[51] *Rasselas*, chap. ix, p. 60.

are always the same." [52] In the Sixtieth *Rambler*, the idea is elaborated and explained: "When the claims of nature are satisfied, caprice, and vanity, and accident, begin to produce discriminations and peculiarities, yet . . . *we are all prompted by the same motives, all deceived by the same fallacies, all animated by hope, obstructed by danger, entangled by desire and seduced by pleasure.*" [53] The antidote to these fallacies, hopes, and desires is the recognition that although we seem to ourselves uniquely different from others, since other men set value upon what does not interest us and have different objectives, the basic motivation which makes them follow their particular objectives and which springs from their essential humanity is identical with ours. This recognition that human nature is uniform will ensure both rationality and Christian humility. It will save us from both subjectivity and pride: "Keep this though *always prevalent, that you are only one atom of the mass of humanity.*" [54]

As anyone will have noticed who has "attentively" read the *Rambler, Rasselas,* the *Vanity of Human Wishes,* the *Preface to Shakespeare,* or the *Lives of the English Poets,* Johnson's main preoccupation is always with time, not in the abstract but as the irreducible mode of human existence. The initial religious concern which underlies all Johnson's morality shows itself in the constant distinction, on many levels, between the temporal "Choice of Life" and the "Choice of Eternity." Generality points to that which is beyond temporal existence precisely because it survives even within time. The partial view, the intensity of a narrow preoccupation, necessarily obscures all other possible views of experience and is therefore ill-treated by time. "It is indeed, the fate of controvertists," we are told in *Rambler* No. 106, "even when they contend for philosophical or theological truth, to be soon laid aside and slighted," [55] whereas the true moralist, whose view is not determined by transient polemics but by his insight into what is most general in human nature, may rationally hope that his writings will survive his death. The occupation of the true moralist (who is the only true poet) has more rational dignity and endurance than that of the specialist in particular sciences because it is concerned with what

[52] *Ibid.,* chap. x, p. 61.
[53] *Works,* II, 287.
[54] *Rasselas,* chap. xlvi, p. 150.
[55] *Works,* III, 4.

does not change: "There are, indeed, few kinds of composition
from which an author, however learned and ingenious, can hope a
long continuance of fame. He who has carefully studied human
nature, and can well describe it, may with most reason flatter his
ambition." [56] Particular and partial observation is thus connected in
Johnson's mind with the elusive and transient and comes to mean
the same thing.

The entire body of his literary criticism rests on this identification
of generality with enduring interest, moral truth, and aesthetic worth.
The crucial notion is again that of "attention;" only that which is
generally true, true for all times and places, will have *interest* for
future generations, whereas the particular will inevitably become
boring once its occasion has passed:

> Of the ancient poets every reader feels the mythology *tedious* and oppressive.
> Of Hudibras, *the manners being founded on opinions, are temporary and local,* and
> therefore become every day less intelligible, and *less striking.* What Cicero
> says of philosophy is true of wit and humour, that "time effaces the fictions
> of opinion, and confirms the determination of Nature." Such manners as
> depend upon *standing relations and general passions* are co-extended with the
> race of man; but those modifications of life, and peculiarities of practice,
> which are the progeny of error and perverseness, or at best of *some*
> *accidental influence or transient persuasion,* must perish with their parents. [57]

Shakespeare's greatness lies above all in his transcendence of such
"accidental influences," which is simultaneously a transcendence
of the limits of particularity and of temporal life. His characters, who

> are not modified by the customs of *particular* places, un-practised by the
> rest of the world . . . or the *accidents* of *transient* fashions or *temporary*
> opinions . . . are the genuine progeny of *common* humanity, such as the
> world will *always* supply, and observation will *always* find. His persons act
> and speak by the influence of those *general* passions and principles by which
> *all* minds are agitated, and the whole system of life is continued in motion.
> In the writings of other poets a character is too often an individual; in those
> of Shakespeare it is commonly a *species.* [58]

We have seen how men's tendency to ascribe absolute value
to their particular pursuits may be redeemed by their rational ability
to relate themselves to the general fabric of society. The narrow
impulses of Imagination become positive when properly regulated
by the wider awareness of Reason. The same balancing of general

[56] *Ibid.,* 5.
[57] *Life of Butler,* in *Lives,* II, 144.
[58] *Preface to Shakespeare, Works,* V, 105–6.

and particular may be observed in most (though not in all) of
Johnson's observations on poetry. The particular fulfills a positive
function in true poetry so long as it remains subservient to the
initial conception of a whole. Thomson is praised for having "a
mind that at once comprehends the vast, and attends to the
minute," [59] and in Johnson's own work the particular commonly
fulfills the function of exemplification, for the natural tendency of
his mind was to generalize from all topics. Even in dealing with so
specialized a subject as the problems facing an editor of Shakespeare
he is immediately led to the comment that "the chief desire of him
that comments an author, is to show how much other
commentators have corrupted and obscured him. The opinions
prevalent in one age, as truths above the reach of controversy, are
confuted and rejected in another, and rise again to reception in
remoter times. Thus the human mind is kept in motion, without
progress." [60] His comments become more and more general as he
pursues his subject. In *Rasselas* we are told that "example is always
more efficacious than precept," [61] and indeed the whole book may be
regarded as a series of ingenious particular exemplifications of
general truths. History, whether of nations or of art, is important
only to the extent that it illustrates general moral truth. [62]

A genre like literary biography is no less moral (that is to say,
dependent on the universal truths it makes us perceive in the
particular instance) than the invented situations in *Rasselas*. In the
Sixtieth *Rambler*, which is partly devoted to an assessment of
biography as a literary form, Johnson writes that "most accounts of
particular persons are barren and useless," [63] because they deal with
the insignificant idiosyncracies of individual life. "The only
circumstance by which Tickell has distinguished Addison from the
the rest of mankind [was] the irregularity of his pulse." But the
facts of biography can become supremely significant when they
embody something profoundly illustrating general human nature:

[59] *Life of Thomson*, in *Lives*, II, 358. Thomson's poem has both a "wide expansion
of design" and an "enumeration of circumstantial details."
[60] *Preface to Shakespeare, Works*, V, 141.
[61] *Rasselas*, chap. xxx, p. 109.
[62] " . . . there is always a silent reference of human works to human abilities . . .
the enquiry, how far *man* may extend his designs, or how high he may rate his
native force, is of far greater dignity than in what rank we shall place *any particular
performance*" (*Preface to Shakespeare, Works*, V, 124).
[63] *Works*, II, 289.

"all the plans and enterprises of De Witt are now of less importance to the world, than that part of his personal character, which represents him as careful of his health, and negligent of his life." [64] In the first few paragraphs of his own *Life of Savage*, Johnson deals in a general way with the typically Johnsonian idea that even those who are aware of the fact that worldly greatness and power do not guarantee happiness frequently expect intellectual greatness to "produce better effects," but this "expectation" is "very frequently disappointed." [65] The narrative of Richard Savage's life is then offered as an illustration, a particular instance, of this sad general truth.

Generality in art, associated with moral truth, reason, and permanence, is also connected in Johnson's mind with the principle of "diversification" or interest. In the first chapter I attempted to show that Johnson's entire moral system proceeds from the observation that the mind in itself, apart from its experience, is in a natural state of vacuity or boredom, which determines its attitude toward all experience. The mind needs to be filled by diverse objects succeeding each other quickly, else it grows restless and uneasy. Imlac, for example, grows bored by the "barren uniformity" of the sea and longs for the land, where there are "mountains and valleys, deserts and cities"; and if nature prove uninteresting, he at least expects to find "variety in life." [66]

Poetry, in order to present its general message, must hold attention, and it can do this only by "filling the mind" during the time-span of the reading with a variety of particular details which in conjunction will form the true experience of a whole. It has perhaps not been sufficiently noticed how central this principle of interest is in Johnson's criticism. Shakespeare's merit does not lie only in the fact that his drama is "the mirror of life" and that the reader who "has mazed his *imagination* in following the *phantoms* which other writers raise before him, may here be cured of his *delirious exstasies, by reading human sentiments in human language.*" [67] It also lies in the simple and all-important fact that Shakespeare's plays are on the whole interesting. In *Romeo and Juliet* "the scenes are busy and

[64] *Ibid.*, 288.
[65] *Life of Savage*, in *Lives*, II, 93.
[66] *Rasselas*, chap. ix, p. 58.
[67] *Preface to Shakespeare*, *Works*, V, 108.

various." [68] In *Troilus and Cressida*, Shakespeare "has diversified his characters with great variety.[69] *Antony and Cleopatra "keeps curiosity always busy, and the passions always interested.* . . . The continual hurry of the action, the variety of incidents, and the quick succession of one personage to another, *call the mind forward without intermission* from the first Act to the last." [70] Thus the great poet simultaneously instructs us by pointing to "general and transcendental truths, which will always be the same" and delights us by making full and diversified use of his knowledge of all particular "modes of life." [71] Just as instruction and delight are separable only in analysis—in the work of art they are simultaneous—so real generality and an interesting heterogeneity of particulars are mutually complementary. Like Imlac, who is "less unhappy . . . because [he has] *a mind replete with images,* which [he] can vary and combine at pleasure," [72] poetry will truly delight only when it is all-embracing both in the sense that its conception has a wide extent covering many particulars at once and in the sense that it ranges from one particular to another with a versatility and inventiveness that leave no gaps of attention.

This principle of variety runs through Johnson's thought on subjects other than poetry, throwing light on his insistence that interest is a *sine qua non* of good art. Nature's real *use*, we are told in the fifth *Rambler* (a meditation on the spring), in addition to the instruction it provides by offering us objects for ethical meditation, lies in its great variety, in the fact that it may provide sane and rational entertainment by feeding our incessant appetite for diversity and novelty.

> There is, indeed, something inexpressibly pleasing in the annual renovation of the world, and the new display of the treasures of nature. . . . The SPRING affords to a mind, so free from the disturbance of cares or passions as to be *vacant to calm amusements,* almost everything that our present state makes us capable of enjoying. The *variegated verdure* of the fields and woods, the succession of grateful odours, the voice of pleasure pouring out its notes on every side . . . throw over the whole earth an air of gaiety significantly expressed by the smile of nature.[73]

[68] *On Shakespeare*, p. 188.
[69] *Ibid.*, p. 184.
[70] *Ibid.*, p. 180.
[71] *Rasselas*, chap. x, p. 63.
[72] *Ibid.*, chap. xii, p. 69.
[73] *Rambler* No. 5, *Works*, II, 22.

Johnson goes on to recommend walks in the spring as good medicine for disturbed, bored, melancholy, and restless minds. The contemplation of nature may be a good antidote to the harmful mental tendency to fix upon a single notion to the exclusion of all others. A man obsessed by his subjective imagination, by his private hopes or fears, will do well to make use of nature, which may bring him back to comparative sanity by providing him with numerous "objects of attention" that are *really there*. Nature, thus approached, may serve as a cure for Imagination by releasing us from our "particular thoughts:"

There are animals that borrow their colour from the neighbouring body, and consequently vary their lure as they happen to change their place. In like manner it ought to be the endeavour of every man to derive his reflections from the objects about him; for it is to no purpose that he alters his position, if *his attention continues fixed to the same point*. The mind should be *kept open to the access of every new idea*, and so far *disengaged from the predominance of particular thoughts*, as easily to accommodate itself to occasional entertainment.[74]

Johnson's various preoccupations may be seen converging in the language of this meditation. Although "a nation of naturalists is neither to be hoped, nor desired," nature can and should provide "fresh amusement" for those who "languish in health and repine in plenty." In brief, for those who are, like the inhabitants of the Happy Valley, bored. Nature's variety and diversity can be good medicine for the mind's obsession with "particular thoughts"— "particular" with all its Augustan connotations of pride, passion, hope and fear, and sin; in the same sense that great poetry counters excessive Imagination. The moral point is in the anti-specialization implied in all Johnson recommends. Swift's mad projectors and Pope's rival botanist and entomologist are so totally involved in the particularities of nature that they become freaks of nature themselves. Johnson's ultimate justification for the study and enjoyment of natural phenomena is precisely in the religious emphasis on the general. It is not "the partial, narrow" aspects of nature that are of interest to a mind in search of sanity and reason, not the "streaks of the tulip" but "the inexhaustible stock of materials" which nature can provide to fill, entertain, instruct, and keep the balance of the mind. A man who forms the habit of turning natural study to

74 *Ibid.*, p. 23.

advantage "has always a certain prospect of discovering new reasons for adoring the sovereign Author of the universe, and probably hopes of making some discovery of benefit to others, or of profit to himself." [75]

What is true of the contemplation of nature is true of the description of nature in poetry and is true of poetry in general. Just as the virtue of nature described in the fifth *Rambler* lies in its "inexhaustible stock of materials," Shakespeare's, discussed in the *Preface*, lies in his "inexhaustible plenty." [76] Great poetry both "fills the eye with awful pomp, and gratifies the mind with endless diversity." [77] The fault of the metaphysical poets lies not so much in their dwelling upon particulars—this in itself may be necessary for the illustration of general truth—as in their conceits, in their tendency to elaborate and "labour particularities" without making them subservient to a wider rational design. Cowley "loses the *grandeur* of generality" by "claiming a dignity" for the detail which only the whole can have. By doing so, he loses all sublimity and indeed becomes "ridiculous." [78] Shakespeare, on the other hand, "opens a mine which contains gold and diamonds in unexhaustible plenty" where "other poets display cabinets of precious rarities, minutely finished." [79]

One may thus distinguish between two kinds of particularity in Johnson's thought. On the one hand, the particular represents those elements in reality, neutral in themselves, which are turned by the Imagination (through its distorting operations of hope, fear, delusive recall, and intellectual "speculation") into static objects of absolute value. These obsessive particulars become substitutes for both observation and thought; a mind riddled with such particularity is incapable of rational activity. The danger of particulars lies in that they limit the mind's perspective, its freedom to exercise itself in the only way that is compatible with the temporal process in which it is placed, through flexible and continuous observation, selection, and rejection. The imaginative faculty increases the inherent incompatibility between the mind's employment and the temporal reality upon which it must be employed if sanity is to be preserved,

[75] *Ibid.*, pp. 23–24.
[76] *Preface to Shakespeare, Works,* V, 127.
[77] *Ibid.*
[78] *Life of Cowley,* in *Lives,* I, 36.
[79] *Preface to Shakespeare, Works,* V, 127.

by limiting individual attention to the detail, the partial goal, and the fixed object (pinned down by imagination, not truly fixed, for nothing within time can be static in itself). The culmination of such partiality is madness, an absolute subjectivity in which time becomes frozen around some partial aspect of experience that excludes attention to all else. But there is another kind of particularity in Johnson's thought that is positive and is in fact the essence of Reason's work. The general arises from moving flexibly handled particulars that are reasoned into law and principle, and such particulars from observation are both healthy and necessary. They form the imaginative basis of all rational cogitation and are the material through which consciousness must work both in life and in art.

Generality too may be seen as either positive or negative, depending on the strength of its relation to the moving particulars that are its guarantee of validity. The attempt to maintain a general point of view that is divorced from concrete particulars is a product of obsessiveness and pride. The futile ambition of the flier and the stoic in *Rasselas* to detach themselves completely from the kind of particularity and limitation inherent in the sublunar state of man, the ambition of the "speculators" in metaphysics or morals or criticism to construct all-embracing systems for which concrete exemplification will be irrelevant, creates a split in their all-too-human consciousness, or paradoxically limits them to ever more negative and constricting narrowness. Their willful divorce from reality may mask itself as Reason, but for Johnson "erring reason" springs from extreme imagination. It should be added that exactly the same distinction between integral and disjointed generality is present in Johnson's application of aesthetic standards. Shakespeare's greatness lies in his ability to convey insight into the general state of mankind by means of vivid and concrete particulars. Nicholas Rowe's plays are "general" indeed, but Johnson condemns them for precisely that reason. They lack "accurate discriminations" and fall flat because everything in them is *"general and indefinite."* [80]

Johnson's central point for the literary critic is an extension of his lesson for all men. Criticism applies criteria of judgment that suffer, like all intellectual constructions, from the fact that they tend

[80] *Life of Rowe*, in *Lives*, II, 76.

to exclude rival criteria and other constructions, of which perforce there are many. Johnson's practice as a critic is consistent with his more general teaching in that he sees literary judgment as perennially open to correction from *life*. His defense of Shakespeare against the critics of "narrower principles," who condemn Shakespeare's mixture of high and low styles and his disregard of the conventional unities, must be understood as an insistence upon open rather than closed critical judgment. What underlies Johnson's evaluation of Shakespeare is the conviction that critical and aesthetic systems are no less a product of Imagination's "speculative" nature than are man's metaphysical attempts to provide a systematic explanation of the universe. Doctrinal criticism (and all critics in some measure are doctrinal) springs from the profoundest of human needs—the need to rest in some absolutely fixed criterion of value and thereby impose an absolute pattern upon the chaotic material of raw experience. Critical judgment, Johnson believed, proceeds from a human and therefore limited viewpoint; to correct this necessary limitation, the critic must at least rationally confront its necessity and be prepared to modify his own private estimate in view of what many men have believed in many ages.

Johnson's ideas of generality and particularity in art, as in life, thus represent a critique of all purely systematic thinking. The touchstone, if critical judgment is to be close to its object, must always be human reality itself and not a set of presuppositions. Humility is as necessary for good criticism as it is for salvation, humility in the sense that we must be prepared to efface our "darling" imaginative schemes when reality does not conform to them. "General" criticism, referring judgment to life, open to the impression of new particulars, able to take in the surprising as well as the conventional, what at first seems outside the accepted sphere of reference as well as what can easily be accounted for, is a true exercise of Reason, partaking of the dignity (and the religious value) that all rational pursuits confer.

Johnson's literary activity itself may serve as a model for the writer who aspires to such generality. The astounding flexibility of mind which he displayed as he moved from one subject to another, equally competent at lexicography, economics, poetry, and a score of other heterogeneous disciplines, is a measure of the generality he not only extolled but practiced. Not many may hope to imitate such breadth of comprehension and versatility of writing, especially in an age that abounds with one-subject professors who do much of the critical revaluation that the age requires. But the humble recognition of limitation, as Johnson so fully illustrates, is in itself a partial transcendence of limitation. The writer, the critic, the scholar, enter a groove of thought and feeling that is determined by what their own particular "attention" finds available in the circumstances of their life, but their release is possible through the self-effacing awareness of this fact. Humanity, constricted by initial choices—conscious or half-conscious—that determine the actual framework within which the world is observed and evaluated, may be saved by glancing at the mirror that truly "general" art puts up to life. The amplitude of Johnson's own generality of interest, embodied in all he wrote, must stand as an enduring rebuke and corrective to those who live and write by "narrower principles."

Finally, it must be emphasized that for Johnson the ultimate justification of fullness and versatility in literary practice lay in religion. My main point in this chapter, as indeed throughout this book, is that his ideas on many seemingly unrelated subjects appear strikingly coherent when we trace them to what is the point of departure of his thought: the religious idea that there is an inherent contradiction between human craving and human employment. Man's potentiality transcends the limits of time and space. The only object which can finally fulfill it must have as infinitely wide an extent as itself, and this is true only of the divine. In all experience Johnson found confirmation for his basic view that the human tragedy lay in the insufficiency of all things circumscribed and ephemeral to a hunger that is limitless and infinite, and his insistence that poetry must go beyond the bounds of the narrow, the detailed, and the particular is an extension of his basic religious presupposition concerning human life.

CHAPTER SIX: THE FOLLY OF UTOPIA

Sir, most schemes of political improvement are very laughable things (Life, II, 102)

*I*n the course of his adventures, Rasselas learns quite a few things about human nature, not the least of which in importance is the absurdity of *Utopia.* In the early chapters we find Rasselas, still completely the naïf, reacting with surprise and indignation when Imlac tells him of the rapacity of certain governors in the provinces. " 'Surely,' said the prince, 'my father must be negligent of his charge, if any man in his dominions dares take that which belongs to another. . . . *If I were emperor,* not the meanest of my subjects should be oppressed with impunity.' " Imlac points out that Rasselas may someday "acquit" his father, since "oppression is, in the Abyssinian dominions, neither frequent nor tolerated; but *no form of government has been yet discovered, by which cruelty can be wholly prevented.*" [1] In the following chapter, as Imlac continues his narrative with an account of the way his traveling companions had taken advantage of his innocence and had exposed him to fraud "without any advantage to themselves, but that of rejoicing in the superiority of their own knowledge," Rasselas is still completely incredulous. "Is there such depravity in man, as that he should injure another without benefit to himself?" Imlac patiently attempts to explain human pride and envy, but Rasselas still will not believe man to be so unreasonable.[2]

Later in the book, having seen something of the world, Rasselas does realize that perfect government is a mirage, because of the necessarily imperfect nature both of the governor and the governed. The first part of his "Disquisition upon Greatness" in Chapter XXVII presumably expresses the viewpoint of experience (i.e., Johnson's own): "He that has much to do will do something wrong

[1] *Rasselas*, chap. viii, p. 55.
[2] *Ibid.*, chap. ix, p. 59.

. . . and if it were possible that he should always act rightly, yet when such numbers are to judge of his conduct, the bad will censure and obstruct him with malevolence, and the good sometimes by mistake." [3] But like all the other lessons which the travelers in the book learn from their experiences, the knowledge that the human condition itself makes nonsense of the notion of a perfect state is held by only part of Rasselas' mind. After Imlac's crucial discourse on "The Dangerous Prevalence of Imagination" in Chapter XLIV, Rasselas confesses to a secret "indulgence of fantastic delight" which he now recognizes as "dangerous":

> I have frequently endeavoured to *image the possibility* of a perfect government, by which all wrong should be restrained, all vice reformed, and all the subjects preserved in tranquility and innocence. This thought *produced innumerable schemes of reformation*, and dictated many useful regulations and salutary edicts. This has been *the sport, and sometimes the labour, of my solitude;* and I start when I think with how little anguish I once supposed the death of my father and my brothers. [4]

Nor is this a final purging of Rasselas' secret ambitions. In the final chapter, the ironical "Conclusion in which Nothing is Concluded," the last we hear of Rasselas is that he "desired a *little* kingdom in which he might administer justice *in his own person*, and see all the parts of government *with his own eyes;* but he could never fix the limits of his dominions, and was always adding to the number of his subjects." [5]

What is the point of this sequence? In the present chapter I should like to show how in his view of the perennial dream of a perfect commonwealth Johnson's religious, moral, psychological, and political views converge. In addition I wish to point out what seem to me enlightening similarities and differences between the satirical utopias in *Rasselas* and those of Sir Thomas More, Swift, and Voltaire.

To begin, we note that in Rasselas' mind the perfect kingdom is inevitably headed by himself. In the early part of the book he sees the possibility of perfect government, "if I were emperor," and in the conclusion he is still dreaming of "administering justice in my own person." The idea of utopia is thus connected with pride or, in

[3] *Ibid.*, chap. xxvii, p. 100.
[4] *Ibid.*, chap. xliv, pp. 141–42.
[5] *Ibid.*, chap. xlix, p. 158.

other words, with the human tendency to see absolute value as residing in the self. Not that Rasselas is in any sense vicious. Inasmuch as one may speak of character in the context of an English *conte philosophique*, where character plays so small a part, Rasselas is a thoroughly admirable young man, constantly trying to get at the truth by experience and heroically attempting to recognize and control his irrational impulses. Yet his utopian impulse does represent Pride, in its most generic sense, the sense in which man— good, bad, or indifferent, simply by virtue of his humanity— madly "expects" in some way to become more than man. The astronomer whose tragic derangement sums up the message of the entire book is of course a supreme example of Pride, yet he is one of the most admirably virtuous "characters" of them all.

I think the late Professor Lovejoy threw most light on this matter when he noted that "pride" in eighteenth-century thought designated (among other things) a " 'passion', or set of passions, which was recognized by many, not to say most, of the more acute literary psychologists of the period as the most powerful and pervasive motive of men's behaviour, the 'spring of action' which differentiates *homo sapiens* from all the other animals, and by which all his most distinctive human propensities and performances, good or bad, are to be explained." [6] Johnson's condemnation of utopia springs from a basic diagnosis of the human condition shared by many medieval and Renaissance moralists (including Shakespeare). Rasselas, secretly dreaming of his perfect commonwealth, epitomizes human pride in that his dream implies a dissatisfaction with the present state of affairs and fixes upon a state in which all actual imperfections are ignored or magically remedied. The idea of utopia presupposes a commonwealth of perfect beings, living in complete harmony with one another, and is therefore in complete opposition to the basic Christian doctrine that man is a fallen and depraved creature who cannot attain perfection on his own. The notion of a perfect earthly state makes nonsense of the Heavenly City, and therefore is seen by Johnson as at root "dangerous" to both religion and morality.

In *Rasselas*, the utopian dream is precisely analogous to the "Artist's" attempt to fly in Chapter VI and the "Wise and Happy"

[6] A. O. Lovejoy, "Pride in Eighteenth-Century Thought," *Essays in the History of Ideas*, (Baltimore, 1948), p. 62.

stoic's belief that man can live by reason alone, unmoved by hope and fear. In all these cases, the underlying motive is man's over-reaching himself, man's tendency to imagine himself with powers which in reality he can never have. In Rasselas' perfect kingdom men are to be "regulated" in the way the mad Astronomer believes he can "regulate" the stars and planets. Like the Astronomer, Rasselas is imagining himself a god.

Thus for Johnson, Montaigne's question, "is it possible to imagine anything so ridiculous as that this puny creature, who is not even master of himself . . . should call himself master,"[7] applies to the political no less than to any other sphere of human activity. It is the basic theme underlying all of Johnson's remarks on human history, whether in *The Vanity of Human Wishes* or in the political pamphlets. Man's dream that he can on his own bring about a frictionless society and in his own person embody perfect Justice is merely another manifestation of that pitiful creature's mad belief that he can be something other than himself. And this belief or hope or expectation, which Johnson saw as the root of many of the criminal acts that make up human history, need not in itself be vicious. On the contrary, its mainspring may be precisely the desire to do good. As Lovejoy put it, Pride in eighteenth-century thought "in an especially important sense, meant a sort of moral overstrain, the attempt to be unnaturally good and immoderately virtuous, to live by reason alone."[8] One does not need to search far in the historical developments of the last two hundred years, in the benevolent ideological roots of modern fanaticism, totalitarianism, and nihilism, to see what Johnson meant when he called the utopian dream "dangerous."

But the idea of Pride in itself does not account for the exposé in *Rasselas*. The notion of Pride, in Johnson as in many before him, becomes truly meaningful only in terms of the complementary concept of Imagination. Rasselas, when confessing "with what little anguish" he imagined the death of his father, says that he tended "to *image* the possibility of a perfect government." Pride, the mainspring of human behavior, leads to wish fulfillment. Such wish fulfillment entails the creation of subjective worlds in which man

[7] *Apology for Raymond Sebond, Complete Essays,* trans. D. M. Frame (New York, 1960), II.

[8] Lovejoy, "Pride in Eighteenth-Century Thought," p. 67.

becomes a creature not limited by the inadequacies of his real
condition. Each character in *Rasselas* instances a different variety of
such "imagination," and one might say that the identification of
Imagination and Pride is a central tenet of Johnson's moral thought.
In *The Vanity of Human Wishes*, Juvenal's short phrase
"remota/erroris nebula"[9] is transmuted into:

> . . . *wav'ring man, betray'd by* vent'rous pride,
> *To tread the dreary paths without a guide,*
> *As treach'rous phantoms in the mist delude,*
> *Shuns* fancied *ills, or chases* airy *good* . . .   (*ll. 7–10*)

Rasselas' dream of a perfect kingdom which he himself in reason
knows to be "dangerous," is precisely such a "treach'rous phantom"
of *imaginative* pride.

Johnson's Christian pessimism is best understood when we note
that of the two contradictory faculties he saw as the basic
constitution of man, Reason (associated with humility and piety) and
Imagination (associated with pride and rebellion), the former's
disclosures are too painful, whereas the latter's are absurd. In the
second *Rambler*, having concluded that without the imaginative
flights of "hope" no human endeavor in the actual world would be
possible, Johnson goes on to point out the quixotic nature of all
temporal life. Life itself implies the absurd madness of subjective
wish fulfillments:

When the knight of La Mancha gravely recounts to his companion the
adventures by which he is to signalize himself in such a manner that he shall
be summoned to the support of empires . . . very few readers, amidst their
mirth or pity, can deny that they have admitted visions of the same kind;
though they have not, perhaps, expected events equally strange, or by means
equally inadequate. When we pity him, we reflect on our own
disappointments; and when we laugh, our hearts inform us that he is not
more ridiculous than ourselves, except that he tells what we have only
thought.[10]

One is reminded of Rasselas (in Chapter IV), completely
engrossed in "visionary bustle," pursuing the nonexistent
persecutors of the nonexistent Lady in Distress. The core of the
entire tale is its manifold underlining of the quixoticism inherent
in all men simply by virtue of their humanity. Not only is the mad

---

[9] Juvenal *Satura* x. 2. 3–4, in *Juvenal and Persius* (Loeb Classical Library), p. 192.
[10] *Rambler* No. 2, *Works*, II, 8.

Astronomer a striking counterpart of Cervantes' knight; each of the travelers harbors his own private quixotic life of imagination and hope. Rasselas and his dream of "a perfect government, by which all wrong should be restrained," at the head of which he sees himself; the princess who has "soothed her thoughts" so often with pastoral reveries of innocence and perfect happiness that she confesses to having actually heard sheep bleating through her window; or her favorite Pekuah who imagines herself Queen of Abyssinia,[11] all demonstrate the same malady. Imlac's discourse on the "dangerous prevalence of imagination" is an explanation in terms of moral psychology of the quixoticism and mad utopianism that characterize all human dreams of perfection, power, and absolute happiness on earth.

The idea of a perfect commonwealth may thus be said to manifest the tragic human tendency to create "projects," which as Johnson said of Swift's *Project for the Advancement of Religion*, "if not generally impracticable, [are] yet evidently hopeless, as [they] suppose more zeal, concord, and perseverance than a view of mankind gives reason for expecting." [12] Utopian projects (Rasselas' "secret dream" produces "innumerable schemes of reformation") involve the basic human desire to be deluded, or rather that necessity of illusion to "happiness" which so many moralists in the humanistic tradition (notably Erasmus in his *Praise of Folly* and Swift in the *Tale of A Tub*) satirized. Johnson saw such illusions as fixations upon impossible future events which are transformed by Imagination to appear as the solutions of all ills. The Perfect Kingdom of Rasselas is entirely analogous to the Jacobitism of "Tom Tempest" satirized in the tenth *Idler*: "He is a steady friend to the house of Stuart, [and] is of the opinion that if the exiled family had continued to reign, there would have neither been worms in our ships nor caterpillars in our trees." [13] Human folly occurs when men give in to the "particular trains of ideas" which "fix the attention," [14] "intrench themselves strongly in the mind," [15] and

---

[11] *Rasselas*, chap. xliv, p. 141.
[12] *Life of Swift*, in *Lives*, II, 191. Johnson, however, did not doubt the "purity of intention" of Swift's plan.
[13] *Works*, IV, 180.
[14] *Rasselas*, chap. xliv, p. 140.
[15] *Rambler* No. 58, *Works*, II, 277

ultimately so weaken the rational faculty—the faculty which
confronts reality for what it is—that complete madness may ensue.

The connection which Johnson makes between Utopia and
Imagination throws light on the striking absence of illusion in his
own periodical essays on political subjects. Underlying all his views
on current affairs is the insistence on a full recognition of strife,
discord, and war as the inevitable attributes of earthly existence and
capable therefore only of partial, never of complete remedy. It is the
basis of his insistence in his literary criticism that any (nonsatirical)
portrayal of men in a perfectly harmonious condition on earth (such
as that of pastoral literature) is a product of escapist fantasy and
does not fulfill the moral function of art. The obstinate refusal to be
led from the difficult but salutary path of Reason into the "mazes"
of Imagination is the basic keynote of the many political pamphlets:
in the *Observations on the State of Affairs in 1756*, for example,
discussing the progress of the Seven Years' War, Johnson comments
that "there are not two nations, confining on each other, between
whom a war may not always be kindled with plausible pretences on
either part, as there is always passing between them a reciprocation
of injuries, and fluctuation of encroachments." [16] In *An Introduction
to the Political State of Great Britain*, the relations between England
and Holland are tough-mindedly explained: "No mercantile man, or
mercantile nation, has any friendship but for money, and alliance
between them will last no longer, than their common safety, or
common profit is endangered; no longer than they have an enemy,
who threatens to take from each more than either can steal from the
other." [17] Perfect political harmony, whether between nations or
within the state, is as unthinkable as a society of angels on earth:
"disagreement of opinion will [exist] *because we are finite beings.*" [18]

Man on earth is a creature *in history*, and the idea of history
itself makes nonsense of the notion of a perfect commonwealth.
Time, the irreducible mode of human life, means change, and change
precludes perfect balance. "In every change, there will be many that
suffer real or imaginary grievances, and therefore, many will be
dissatisfied." [19] Man's temporal nature *is* his fallen state. A rational

[16] *Literary Magazine*, XI (July–Aug., 1756), *Works*, VI, 118–9.
[17] *Literary Magazine*, I (1756), *Works*, VI, 136.
[18] *Adventurer* No. 107, *Works*, IV, 95.
[19] *Ibid.*, 129.

recognition of the fact that "he that runs against time has an antagonist not subject to casualties" [20] and that "nothing terrestrial can be kept at a stand" [21]—a fact wilfully ignored by Imagination and Pride—is a sufficient antidote to utopian hopes; as is an awareness that "the depravity of mankind is so easily discoverable, that nothing but the desert or the cell can exclude it from notice. . . . What are all the records of history, but narratives of successive villanies, of treasons and unsurpations, massacres and wars?" [22] A confrontation and acceptance of such bitter truths should make us wary of all radical schemes of reformation and lead us to adopt a rational or skeptical conservatism as opposed to "visionary" or "metaphysical" [23] political positions—whether conservative or progressive. Inasmuch as Johnson had faith in a social creed, it was his tacit acceptance, along with many of his contemporaries both Tory and Whig, of Locke's views concerning the conservative underpinning of the British political system. But what is more fundamental in Johnson's political stance is the extreme distrust with which he held *all* political theories as well as all far-reaching political and economic projects. His skeptical rejection of utopian pride is what underlies the *Further Thoughts on Agriculture* and *Considerations on Corn*. It explains his objections in 1756 to the Seven Years' War, the attitudes he expressed in *Taxation no Tyranny*, and the doubts he constantly entertained about the growing tendency in English politics to abandon the older conception of a self-sufficient Little England in favor of grandiose plans to master world commerce through imperial expansion. Anyone who finds his position negative must be reminded that Johnson's skeptical traditionalism is an expression of his humanitarian and egalitarian tendencies. It was Johnson, not the "patriots," who took the side of the underdog, whether Negro slave, American Indian, or Hebridean crofter.

The method of *Rasselas* is the method of satire, in the sense that it involves an ironical exposé of human delusions which is intended to make us confront unpleasant realities. By means of its irony, it

---

[20] *Life of Pope*, in *Lives*, II, 244.
[21] *Rambler* No. 85, *Works*, II, 399.
[22] *Rambler* No. 175, *Works*, III, 322.
[23] The distinction between the "skeptical" and the "visionary" kinds of conservatism is illuminatingly discussed by Donald J. Greene, *The Politics of Samuel Johnson* (New Haven, Conn., 1960) p. 253. See also Greene's Introduction to the volume devoted to Johnson in the "Twentieth Century Views" Series (Englewood Cliffs, N. J., 1965), esp. pp. 3–4.

makes us see the absurdity of many "luscious falsehoods" and feeds us the salutary "bitterness of truth." If we understand, as Johnson most certainly did, man in general to be a "forward fool," Johnson's lines *To a Young Lady on her Birth-Day*, sum up the basic moral intention of *Rasselas:* "With his own form [to] acquaint the forward fool/Shewn in the faithful glass of ridicule" (ll. 15–16). And it should be noted that the first "luscious falsehood" exposed to the peculiarly Johnsonian mixture of compassion and ridicule is a kind of utopia, a bountiful, leisurely place in which "nothing can be wanted." The Happy Valley is so perfectly ordered that its inhabitants are not expected to desire change. The unmasking of this earthly paradise occupies the entire early section of the book, for, as we progressively learn, the paradise is really a prison, and its inhabitants viciously bored rather than happy. The idea of utopia runs counter to the *necessity of action* which Johnson saw as one of the basic lessons to be learned from the fact that man exists in time.[24]

Throughout his writings, whether moral, political, or aesthetic, the idea that the static condition is unnatural to man is ever-present. In the *Observations on the State of Affairs in 1756*, we learn that not the least of the French motives in colonizing Canada was *"that impatience of doing nothing*, to which mankind, perhaps, owe much of what is imagined to be effected by more splendid motives."* [25] Such statements provide Johnson's fundamental explanation both of the fact that man does dream of earthly paradises and of the fact that a perfect society is a mirage. Johnson was certainly not alone in his recognition of the basic necessity for change and movement in human life. Pascal, with whose thought, as we have seen, Johnson's has much in common, noted that "Rien n'est si insupportable à l'homme que d'être dans un plein repos, sans passions, sans affaire, sans divertissement, sans application. Il sent alors son néant, son abandon, son insuffisance, sa dépendence, son impuissance, son vide. Incontinent, il sortira du fond de son âme l'ennui, la noirceur, la tristesse, le chagrin, le dépit, le désespoir." [26] This is precisely what happens to the inhabitants of the Happy Valley, except that their despair is secret and therefore all the more dangerous. Johnson's

---

[24] See Chapter 1, n. 59.
[25] *Works*, VI, 129.
[26] *Pensées sur la Religion*, 160–[121–131], p. 147. Cf. 163–746[–129]: "Notre nature est dans le movement; le repos entier est la mort" (p. 147).

archfoe Hume also remarked that "there is no craving or demand of the human mind more constant and insatiable than that for exercise and employment" and that this desire seems "the foundation of most of our desires and pursuits,"[27] but he did not draw significant general conclusions from this fact. What is characteristically Johnsonian is the insistent awareness of the political and historical implications of man's hunger for novelty and diversity.

Johnson was most certainly a traditionalist in his politics as in other spheres. His political axioms, like all else in his thought, represent a rethinking in his own terms of the Christian-Humanist heritage. Yet, although Johnson's use of the notion of the mind's "infinite hunger" to expose to ridicule all utopian dreams of static happiness is rooted in the basic tenets of Christianity, it may also be seen as a prefiguration of Nineteenth-century philosophies of Will. Schopenhauer's pessimism may be different from Johnson's in that it does not explicitly root itself in Christianity (although Schopenhauer had a strong appreciation of the Christian negation of the world),[28] but the similarity is more than superficial: "The will can just as little cease from willing altogether on account of some particular satisfaction, as time can end or begin; for it there is no such thing as a permanent fulfillment which shall completely and forever satisfy its craving. It is a vessel of Danaïdes; for it there is no highest good, no absolute good, but always a merely temporary good."[29] Johnson would have agreed perfectly, except for adding, good Christian that he was, that "highest good" and "absolute good" are indeed absurd in any historical context, but hardly so when considered as the *other* state of being opened up by the "Choice of Eternity." As for the "Choice of Life," we learn in *Rambler* No. 103 that "all the attainments possible in our present state are evidently inadequate to our capacities of enjoyment . . . the gratification of one desire encourages another: and after all our labours, studies, and inquiries,

---

[27] David Hume, "Of Interest," *Essays 1740–41* (World's Classics; London), p. 309.
[28] See *World as Will*, in *The Philosophy of Schopenhauer* (New York, 1928), p. 269: ". . . *optimism*, when it is not merely the thoughtless talk of such as harbour nothing but words under their low foreheads, appears not merely as an absurd, but also as a really *wicked* way of thinking, as a bitter mockery of the unspeakable suffering of mankind. Let no one think that Christianity is favourable to optimism; for, on the contrary, in the Gospels world and evil are used as almost synonymous."
[29] *Ibid.*, p. 291.

we are continually at the same distance from the completion of our
schemes, have still some wish importunate to be satisfied, and some
faculty restless and turbulent for want of its enjoyment."

The Happy Valley, then, shows us the foolishness of thinking
that contentment, balance, and perfect harmony can (or indeed
should) be achieved this side of death. A long tradition of
Cockaignes and other false paradises lies behind it, and it has even
been shown that the placing of earthly paradises in Abyssinia was
common literary practice throughout the centuries.[30] What has
perhaps not been sufficiently noted is the indebtedness of Johnson's
satire in *Rasselas* to the satirical tradition engendered by the original
Utopia.[31] More's Utopians had served a double purpose. On the one
hand, they do embody a desirable state, for they have achieved the
perfection of Reason and are not subject to the impulses of what
Johnson termed Imagination. With their vague, tolerant deism, they
exemplify a life of virtue and justice. They are men who have become
as perfect as mere rationality can make men be, for they embody the
four virtues which, as the Middle Ages largely believed, could be
achieved without the aid of faith.[32] In their heathen state, they do
not have the *Christian* virtues of Hope, Faith, and Charity, but
potentially they are quite capable of reaching the perfection of all
seven virtues, since we see them readily embracing Christianity—or
at any rate an extremely liberal interpretation of it—when they hear
of Christ's "doctrine, laws, miracles, and of the no less wonderful
constancy of so many martyrs." [33] But there is nothing more
heterodox in More's *Utopia* than there is in Johnson's *Rasselas*. The
Utopians are a very special breed of *unfallen* humans. More makes

[30] The tradition of the earthly paradise has been studied by G. Boas and A. O.
Lovejoy, *A Documentary History of Primitivism and Related Ideas [in Antiquity]*; G.
Boas, *Essays on Primitivism and Related Ideas in the Middle Ages*; L. Whitney,
*Primitivism and the Idea of Progress in English Popular Literature of the Eighteenth
Century* (Boston, 1934); and H. R. Patch, *The Other World* (Boston, 1950). G. J.
Kolb, in his essay "The Structure of *Rasselas*," *PMLA*, LXVI (1951), p. 703, notes
that the practice of Milton, Johnson, Coleridge, and others indicates that
Abyssinia was a common setting for English descriptions of the earthly paradise
from the 17th to the 19th centuries.

[31] Johnson's forceful arguments against hereditary slavery were probably
reinforced by his reading of *Utopia*. See *Life*, III, 202 and n. 3. The Greek epigram
he composed on More and Erasmus bears witness to his admiration. See *Life*, V,
430.

[32] See R. W. Chambers, "The Meaning of Utopia," in *Thomas More* (London,
1963), p. 118 f.

[33] "Of the Religions in Utopia," *Utopia* (Everyman Library ed.; New York, 1910),
Book II, p. 118.

it clear that the real difference between them and Europeans lies in their prelapsarian freedom from Pride—precisely the human trait Johnson is most concerned to expose in his satire. "Why should it be thought," More asks, "that man would ask more than enough which is sure never to lack? Certainly in all kinds of living creatures fear of lack doth cause covetousness and ravin, or in man *only pride*, which counteth it a glorious thing to pass and excell other in the superfluous and vain ostentation of things. *The which kind of vice among the Utopians can have no place.*" [34] More's primary purpose is thus in reality no less satirical than Johnson's. As Émile Dermenghem put it, "il ne faudrait pas, en effet, s'illusioner sur le véritable sens de l'*Utopie*. Il ne s'agit pas tant d'un tableau de la société idéale que d'un portrait satirique . . . de l'Angleterre et de l'Europe contemporaines." [35] And, one might add, on a deeper level of satire an indirect portrait of the *fallen state* of European man.

By portraying heathen virtue, More has exposed Christian vice, and one can find more than one instance of the same device in the eighteenth-century genre of satirical utopias to which I think Johnson's Happy Valley belongs. Swift's are perhaps the most striking of these. Gulliver himself, after his extended discovery of man's fallen state has driven him mad, is a hopeless utopian. In the "Letter from Captain Gulliver to his cousin Sympson" which prefaces the travels, he complains that his book has not "produced one single effect according to [his] intentions": "I desired you would let me know by a letter, when party and faction were extinguished: judges learned and upright . . . the physicians banished; the female *Yahoos* abounding in virtue, honour, truth and good sense, courts and levees of great ministers thoroughly weeded and swept. It must be owned, that seven months were a *sufficient time to correct* every vice and folly to which *Yahoos* are subject."

It is no wonder that he entertains such irrational expectations after what he has been through. All four voyages abound in mock utopias that serve the double purpose of showing how imperfect European institutions actually are, when measured against an ideal commonwealth, and how absurd the very notion of an ideal, rationally ordered society appears when one considers what human nature is

[34] "Of their Living and Mutual Conversation together," *ibid.*, p. 69.
[35] Émile Dermenghem, *Thomas Morus et les Utopistes de la Renaissance* (Paris, 1927), pp. 103–4.

like. In Lilliput "there are some laws and customs . . . very peculiar,
and if they were not so directly contrary to those of my own dear
country, I should be tempted to say a little in their justification. . . .
All crimes against the state are severely punished. They look upon
fraud as a greater crime than theft. . . . Whoever can there bring
sufficient proof that he hath strictly observed the laws of his
country . . . hath a claim to certain privileges," (etc.); Lilliputian
methods of education, the "public nurseries" described at great
length in Chapter VI, are a parody of Plato's *Republic*. The perfection
of Lilliput's institutions is complemented by certain grotesquely ideal
traits in the Brobdingnagians: "The learning of this people is very
defective, consisting only in morality, history, poetry, and
mathematics, wherein they must be allowed to excel. But the last of
these is wholly applied to what may be useful in life, to the
improvement of agriculture, and all mechanical arts." [36] The science
of the Laputans in Book III is the precise opposite of this, and their
commonwealth is in consequence a reverse utopia, an epitome of
government at it worst. But the mock utopianism, the exposé of
"schemes or perfect felicity," recurs in the same book in the
Academy of Lagado, for example, in the project for the abolishing of
words and their substitution by things to be carried in a bundle on
one's back. One of the advantages of this plan, we are told, is "that
it would serve as a universal language to be understood in all
civilized nations, whose goods and utensils are generally of the same
kind. . . . And thus ambassadors would be qualified to treat with
foreign princes or ministers of state, to whose tongues they were
utter strangers." [37]

In the Struldbrug episode, probably the most explicitly Christian
in the book (and reminiscent of more than one element in *Rasselas*),
Gulliver, upon hearing about the possibility of eternal life, has
expectations no less grotesque than those of the Lagado projectors:
"I should then see the discovery of the longitude, the perpetual
motion, the universal medicine, and many other great inventions
brought to the utmost perfection." [38] And if many of the projects of
Lagado are grotesque because they aim at a perfection alien to the
state of man, the perfection of utopia, the land of the rational horses

[36] *Gulliver's Travels*, Book II, chap. vii.
[37] *Ibid.*, Book III, chap. v.
[38] *Ibid.*, chap. x.

is utopia itself, managed with all the double- and triple-edged
sarcasm of which Swift was master. The Platonic perfection of the
"admirable" Houyhnhnms, their totally harmonious society in which
absolute Justice is realized, does indeed serve to rebuke human
disharmony and perversion, but at the same time it is in itself
grotesque, cold, forbidding, and inhuman. Gulliver, who identifies
himself with those "superior" beings (being horses, they are of
course also inferior beings) goes completely mad at the end of the
book. His madness is Pride: the expectation that human society and
human behavior can be identical with those of the Houyhnhnms.
Much of the satire on human fanaticism and perfectionism in
Gulliver's Travels becomes clearer when we remember Swift's remark
in *The Mechanical Operation of the Spirit*, that "the philosopher's
stone . . . the squaring of the circle . . . Utopian Commonwealths
. . . . all serve for nothing else but to employ or amuse [the] grain
of enthusiasm dealt into every composition."

Thus one of Swift's satirical points in *Gulliver's Travels* is
identical with Johnson's satire on Rasselas' dream of a perfect
kingdom. For Swift, as for Johnson, the idea that man can create
for himself a perfect society is ridiculous. The reason for this
similarity of attitude lies in the Christian-Humanist definition of
human inadequacy shared by both writers,[39] which goes far to
explain the similarity in their general political stance. And the
similarity of attitude frequently accounts for a similarity of method:
Johnson could be as savagely satirical in his treatment of the idea of
"perfect beings" and "superior creatures" as Swift. The description
of Jenyns's superior race of beings, "delight [ing] in the operations of
an asthma, as a human philosopher in the effects of the air pump" [40]
is reminiscent in both tone and intention of the Houyhnhnms' plan
to castrate the Yahoos[41] and of many other Swiftian devices. In
both cases the object of ridicule is the idea of rational perfection
man conceives when he gives free rein to his "presumptuous
imagination," [42] to his "power of forming ideal pictures," as Johnson
defined Imagination in the *Dictionary*.

[39] Despite the fact that Johnson saw the *Travels* as "a book written in open
defiance of truth and regularity" and found Book IV "disgusting." *Life of Swift*, in
Lives, II, 204. The "colour" of Swift's style is "gay, but the substance slight."
Thraliana, I, 172.
[40] *Works*, VI, 64–65.
[41] *Gulliver's Travels*, Book IV, chap. ix.
[42] *Review of A Free Enquiry*, *Works*, VI, 59.

Voltaire's Eldorado—perhaps the best known of eighteenth-century utopias—has frequently been set beside Johnson's Happy Valley, but the relatively superficial similarities between *Candide* and *Rasselas* have blinded critics to the deeply antithetical intentions of the two books. J. W. Krutch, in his study of Johnson, remarks that "the conclusion of *Candide* ('Let us cultivate our garden') would be almost as appropriate to *Rasselas*," [43] and Basil Willey concludes that "*Candide* teaches much the same moral as *Rasselas*." [44] This is quite untrue.

There is an obvious similarity between *Candide* and *Rasselas* in that both are primarily satirical in intention.[45] The primary moral end in both is to explode pretty bubbles and reveal bitter truths. The motto of both could have been Swift's "yesterday I saw a woman flayed, and you will hardly believe how much it altered her appearance for the worse" [46] or Johnson's own statement in the Tenth *Rambler* that "the torch of truth shews much that we cannot, and all that we would not see. In a face dimpled with smiles, it has often discovered malevolence and envy, and detected under jewels and brocade the frightful forms of poverty and distress." [47] Both works are anti-intellectual in the sense that they extol experience of real life and ridicule metaphysical "speculation" of various kinds, especially the kind of speculation that leads to complacent optimism. In both books there is a distrust of the visionary and fanatical side of man. Both recommend action and a rational contact with the reality of life.

But how different the meaning of *action* is in *Rasselas* and *Candide!* For Voltaire in *Candide*, laudable action, the improvement of our lot in this world, implies active combat against the superstitions of a dying order that are the cause of tyranny, war, and ignorance. *Candide* does show us that all intellectual "systems" are false and dangerous and that life is by no means as "good" as the so-called philosophers would have us believe. Like Voltaire's other great attack on philosophical optimism, the *Poème sur le désastre de*

---

[43] J. W. Krutch, *Samuel Johnson* (New York, 1944), p. 183. Cf., Voitle, *Samuel Johnson, The Moralist*, p. 157 f.

[44] B. Willey, *The Eighteenth-Century Background* (London, 1957), p. 49.

[45] For Johnson's acknowledgment of the similarity between *Rasselas* and *Candide* in "plan and conduct" see *Life*, I, 342.

[46] *Tale of a Tub*, sec. IX, p. 110.

[47] *Works*, II, 47.

Lisbonne, it reflects a "painful awareness of . . . an illogical, capricious reality,"[48] but ultimately its message *is* optimistic, in the sense that it is hopefully forward-looking. Voltaire's final injunction that man act to improve his lot in this world is an expression of his meliorism—his belief that patient combat in the cause of tolerance and reason against the tyranny, the ignorance, and the superstition of the old order will finally serve to usher in the new. "Il faut cultiver notre jardin" allegorically points to the "horticultural" efforts of the *Encyclopédie* group who aspired toward the distant Eldorado,[49] and the message of the entire book is summed up by its definite conclusion.

For Voltaire's perfect commonwealth itself must be understood in the light of the book's ending. This ideal land of liberty, plenty, harmony, and *happiness* is of course quite close in spirit to More's conception, as indeed are many of its descriptive details. The entire Eldorado section is in a sense tongue-in-cheek: this exotic land is "le pays où tout va bien: car il faut absolument qu'il y en ait un de cette espéce."[50] Just as More's *Second Book* serves as a satirical exposé of the first, Voltaire's Eldorado is an exposé of his Westphalia and his "World." The playful, satirical note may be detected throughout the description. Yet Voltaire's Eldorado is in addition a "real" utopia in the sense in which More's or Swift's or Johnson's are not. It is an ideal to be literally followed and imitated by European man in the hope that some day reason will triumph and the *earthly* paradise attained. One need only compare it with Swift's Laputa (for as in the Flying Island, the King's "palais des sciences" is "toute pleine d'instruments de mathematique et de physique"[51]) or with Johnson's Happy Valley ("la sortie est bien difficile. . . . Les

---

[48] André Morize in his edition of *Candide* (Paris, 1913), remarks that Candide's garden injunction is "un conseil de travail et d'effort" (p. 223, n. 1; xlvii). Gustave Lanson paraphrased the book's conclusion as: "Raisonner sur la métaphysique ne sert à rien: l'action pratique doit se substituer à la creuse spéculation" (*Voltaire* [Paris, 1910], pp. 151–52.) W. F. Bottiglia, "Voltaire's Garden," *PMLA*, LXVI (1951), 733, shows that "Voltaire considered the metaphor of the garden particularly applicable to the work of the Encyclopaedists, and as such interchangeable with the Biblical figure of the vineyard, for theirs was a sacred mission." Cf., André Bellesort, *Essai sur Voltaire* (Paris, 1925), p. 266: Voltaire's Garden "[n'a] point de frontières." The injunction is certainly not to retreat from public action or general moral involvement; rather, it is to work along the lines of one's real competence and not seek too many adventures.

[49] Boltiglia, "Voltaire's Garden," p. 718.

[50] *Candide*, chap. xvii, in *Romans et Contes* (Paris, 1960), p. 177.

[51] *Ibid.*, p. 180.

montagnes qui entourent tout mon royaume ont dix mille pieds de hauteur, et sont droites comme des murailles" [52]) to see the great spiritual gulf that separated the moralists on both sides of the Channel. The utopias of Swift and Johnson are first and foremost grotesqueries, mock utopias, Christian exposés of the very idea of human perfection or perfectibility. Voltaire's is a real utopia in the sense that it foreshadows what became perhaps the central European dream of the following two centuries—the divinely equitable society of divinely perfect men.

Voltaire's Eldorado, in short, is the true Happy Valley. Johnson's, in which "the blessings of nature were collected, and its evils extracted and excluded," [53] turns out to be the seat of profound unhappiness, a kind of hell in fact. In Johnson's Happy Valley, "every art was practised to make [the sons and daughters of Abyssinia] *pleased with their own condition*," [54] but all such "arts" are doomed to failure. Johnson's Happy Valley stands for the distant ideal which once realized can satisfy no longer. It is beyond all strife and discord, secluded from the real world where "man preys upon man," but it is seen by Rasselas (who in a sense is Everyman) as a place of captivity. Rasselas expects "happiness" to reside in the outside world just as the inhabitants of the outside world imagine perfect bliss to reside in this prison. This is the real function of Johnson's mock utopia: those who are within wish to leave it, those outside wish to enter. Gwyn Kolb has noted that Segged in *Rambler* Nos. 204 and 205 "concentrates his efforts to find happiness in an earthly paradise [whereas] Rasselas, miserable in such a paradise, examines the possibilities for pleasure in the outside world." [55] The reason for this is that the Happy Valley and the "Choice of Life" are merely two satirical devices intended to expose the most basic truths of human existence, the one *seeming* utterly desirable from the distorted viewpoint of the other. As states of being which Imagination, from its convenient distance, gilds and glamorizes to represent the absolute fulfillment of its needs, they are in fact interchangeable. And this interchangeability is the main point Johnson is making in both the Segged *Ramblers* and in *Rasselas*: that

[52] *Ibid.*, pp. 180–1.
[53] *Rasselas*, chap. i, p. 38.
[54] *Ibid.*, chap. ii, p. 40.
[55] Kolb, "The Structure of *Rasselas*," p. 701.

all conditions of existence in time are in the deepest sense equally unsatisfactory, all human wishes profoundly "vain."

This deep pessimism that is the core of *Rasselas* has no paralel in Voltaire. Voltaire thought of Johnson (among other things) as "a superstitious dog" [56] and indicated his incomprehension of what Johnson was getting at when he wrote Madame Bélot that *Rasselas* was a work "d'une philosophie aimable." [57] It is also not surprising that when Boswell asked Johnson whether he thought Voltaire was as bad a man as Rousseau, Johnson answered that it was "difficult to settle the proportion of iniquity between them." [58]

What Voltaire failed to comprehend when he approved of *Rasselas* was its deeply Christian *memento quod es homo*. The entire message of the book could be summed up as: "Nor think the doom of man reversed for thee." [59] *Rasselas* exposes the many ways in which man "amuses desires with impossible enjoyments, and *confers upon his pride unattainable dominion*" (Chap. XLIV). This is supremely the case of man's utopian "expectation." The difference between *Candide* and Johnson's Christian tale is perhaps most manifest in Voltaire's belief that Utopia is ultimately within human grasp and Johnson's conviction that Utopia is a dangerous mirage of "presumptuous" Imagination. Saintsbury was certainly closer than Voltaire to the book's essence when he remarked that "except *Ecclesiastes, Rasselas* is probably the wisest, though with that same exception it is probably the saddest book ever written." [60]

---

[56] *Life*, I, 435.
[57] *Ibid.*, II, 500.
[58] *Ibid.*, 12. Johnson, however, did think that *Candide* "had more power in it than anything Voltaire had written." *Life*, I, 356.
[59] *The Vanity of Human Wishes*, l. 154.
[60] George Saintsbury, *The Peace of The Augustans* (London, 1916), p. 160.

CHAPTER SEVEN: THE RATIONALITY OF FAITH

*T*he two primordial events of *Christianity are the Apple and the Cross.* As descendants of Adam we are all marked by his initial fall from grace, and this is the distinguishing mark of our humanity. Man's inherent unworthiness, his radical limitation when on his own, the taint of his earthly existence, are signified by the Genesis tale which is the major premise of religious experience. The human proclivity to do what is wrong and to believe what is false is not an accident of individual life but is man's most fundamental trait.

As indicated earlier in this book, what Johnson meant by Imagination becomes fully significant only in terms of his Christian conception of man as a creature fallen from grace. One might say that the only human being ever to have lived free of "fancy" in the Johnsonian sense was Adam before his lapse, for the moment the serpent's suggestion of unrealized infinite possibilities led to the tasting of forbidden fruit, Imagination became an integral part of human life. From the Christian point of view, it was Pride, man's secret wish to become something more than man, which underlay the coveting of the Apple; just as Lucifer, the archetype of Pride, had wished to become something more than a mere angel. Satan is the creature of pure Imagination, his whole being determined by the passionately conceived image of himself as what he is not. His imaginative pride is thus the cause of his eternal anguish. Man's analogous Pride, or, interchangeably, his analogous Imagination, is what condemns him to continual "uneasiness." [1] Fallen existence, civilized existence, is forever marked by the futile attempt to bridge the unbridgeable gap between the finite reality of a *creature*, and the idea of absolute, uncreaturely existence; between the felt limitation

---

[1] Cf., *Rambler* No. 128, *Works,* III, 108: "every part of life has its uneasiness," and Johnson's remark that savages, like bears, are not above but below "mental uneasiness" (*Life*, II, 73).

of ephemeral experience and the possibility of some fixed earthly "happiness" invented by delusive fancy. This creatureliness of man is his tragedy. It is also his potential for regeneration.

For if the legend of the Apple accounts for man's Imagination, the Cross is the secret of his Reason, and the Cross is meaningless apart from the Apple. Man's passions draw him to the "Choice of Life," but he is no less capable of the "Choice of Eternity." The striking similarity between the thought of Johnson and that of Pascal is accounted for quite simply by the fact that the Apple and the Cross are at the root of both their diagnoses. Obsessed with the partial and narrow, deluded by earthly hope and fear, condemned to the passionate pursuit and avoidance of ultimately futile ends, man is also capable of taking the "extensive view," paradoxically disengaging himself from his "darling schemes" while still following them. He does so by noting their import *sub specie aeternitatis*. Moving through the mists of earthly hope and fear, man becomes capable of religious hope and fear—the ultimate tests of rationality. Johnsonian man is a son of Adam in that his primary impulse is toward selfishness and pride, toward faction, disagreement, excess, particularity, romantic escape, illusion, obsession, ultimate madness. But he is also potentially saved, for the faculty of reason in him, exercised through initial free choice, makes possible moral commitment, humility (in the widest religious sense), patience, realism, fulfillment of duty, "usefulness," salvation.

The analogy between the Christian concept of actually sinful, potentially redeemed man, and Johnson's analysis of life in terms of the polar faculties of Imagination and Reason, becomes clear only when we realize the mutual dependence of the antithetical terms in each case. Salvation necessitates an acute awareness of sin: it cannot occur where it is not needed in the first place. No medieval sermon, no poem by Donne or Herbert, concentrates unambiguously on salvation; the drama of salvation lies precisely in the possibility that it may not be forthcoming. Christ's gentle face becomes effective only when the question is asked, when the possibility of being "adjudged unto hell" is completely vivid. Apple and Cross are dialectically related in that the Fall itself is "fortunate"—it was Adam's sin that made Christ's sacrifice possible. The repentant Christian must therefore carefully walk the tightrope between the two poles: exclusive concentration upon sin leads to Faustian despair, a denial of God's power to forgive, hence a proud glorification of the self;[2] whereas a concentration upon the love of God so exclusive as to indicate the forgetfulness of His righteous Wrath, His Justice, and His hatred of Sin leads to human self-righteousness, to a self-sufficiency and "security" which is in turn a primary form of damning pride. The condition of redemption is a delicate balance between the presumption of doubt and the presumption of assurance, between the sense of unworthiness and the knowledge of how worth may be achieved.

The same holds true of Johnson's moral analysis. Johnson's apparent pessimism ends up as a paradox of the Fortunate Imagination. Man *must* be imaginative, in the human sense, in order to realize his potential of rationality. Imagination indicates fallenness from grace, in the distorted and partial nature of its perspective, in the way it blinds man to the true state of his affairs. It is human transcendence carried to absurd conclusions, transience falsely transformed into the appearance of eternity. Future and past, the realms of transcendence, become scenes of subjective glamor or horror. And yet Imagination is as necessary an ingredient of life as Reason: Johnson's concept of "hope" could be taken as the supreme example of this. Earthly hope, as we have seen in earlier chapters, is fundamentally absurd. Generated by "the vacuity of life," a mere subjective forward-projection of the imagining mind, it is described in the *Lines on the Death of Dr. Robert Levet* as a "delusive mine," and in *The Vanity of Human Wishes* as the pursuit of "airy good." But this is not the full account. Johnson places no less emphasis on the fact that without hope of one kind or another life itself would become unbearably "stagnant." Imlac's positive therapeutic treatment of Nekayah is in essence an attempt to make her *hope* once again; this theme is central in Johnson's moral pamphlets:

> The mind of man is never satisfied with the objects immediately before it, but is always breaking away from the present moment, and losing itself in schemes of future felicity. . . . This quality of looking forward into futurity seems *the unavoidable condition* of a being, whose motions are gradual and whose life is progressive: as his powers are limited, he must use means

[2] See my essays "Religious Despair in Mediaeval Literature and Art," *Mediaeval Studies*, XXXI (1964), pp. 231–56; "The Religious Despair of Doctor Faustus," *Journal of English and Germanic Philology*, LXIII (1964), 625–47; and "Religious Despair in 'Richard III'," *Romanica et Occidentalia, Etudes dédiées à la mémoire de H. Peri* (Jerusalem, 1963), pp. 234–45.

for the attainment of his ends, and intend first what he performs last; as by continual advances from his first stage of existence, he is perpetually varying the horizon of his prospects, he must always discover new motives of action, new excitements of fear and allurements of desire.[3]

Even the most absurd hope is in fact a kind of blessing:

There is no temper so generally indulged as hope: other passions operate by starts on particular occasions, or in certain parts of life; but hope begins with the first power of comparing our actual with our possible state, and attends us through every stage and period, always urging us forward to new acquisitions, and holding out some distant blessing to our view, promising us either relief from pain, or increase of happiness.

Hope is necessary in every condition. The miseries of poverty, of sickness, of captivity, would, without this comfort, be unsupportable; nor does it appear that the happiest lot of terrestrial existence can set us above the want of this general blessing; or that life, when the gifts of nature and of fortune are accumulated upon it, would not still be wretched, were it not elevated and delighted by the expectation of some new possession, of some enjoyment yet behind, by which the wish shall be at last satisfied, and the heart filled up to its utmost extent.

Hope is, indeed, very fallacious, and promises what it seldom gives; but its promises are more valuable than the gifts of fortune, and it seldom frustrates us without assuring us of recompensing the delay by a greater bounty.[4]

Hope, the mark of man's temporal, fallen, and limited nature, the product of his Imagination, is thus simultaneously both positive and negative, a necessary element of sanity and yet ultimately an aspect of human folly. Reason, too, which at first glance had appeared quite simply the antithesis of Imagination, is not a clear-cut concept. Our previous definition of Reason, as the salutary faculty which decreases the gap between transcendence and actuality, must be qualified, for the critical operation of Reason is dependent upon the impulses of Imagination as the governor is dependent on the governed. Reason brings man down to earth, enables him to face reality and to experience the full urgency of life; it checks the mind's wild flights and bridges the gulf between observation and idea, experience and thought; but no human rationality can operate in a vacuum. The Johnsonian ideal of passionate intelligence would be utterly pointless in a condition of harmonious Being; in the condition, that is, of an angel or a beast. The human potential of Reason is realized through process, not through stasis. Reason is a

---

[3] *Rambler* No. 2, *Works*, II, 6–7.
[4] *Rambler* No. 67, *Works*, II, 317–18.

contingent, not an absolute, struggle to direct and channelize the unquiet promptings of fancy. The rational tendency to check mental unruliness, to confront alienation, and to achieve relative objectivity through contact with the minds of others, has for its materials precisely those of Imagination, the given materials of experience-in-time.

Again, temporal hope could serve as the example. Fanciful and rational earthly hope are different only in degree. Rational lucidity does not negate hope; it merely makes hope more realistic and "difficult," hence more valuable. Within the general conglomeration of possible "vain wishes," Reason selects the least escapist route and the most worthwhile objects of pursuit. In the vision recounted in *Rambler* No. 67, Johnson observes

> that the entrance into the garden of hope was by two gates, one of which was kept by reason, and the other by fancy. Reason was surly and scrupulous, and seldom turned the key without many interrogatories, and long hesitation; but fancy was a kind and gentle portress, she held her gate wide open, and welcomed all equally to the district under her superintendency; so that the passage was crowded by all those who either feared the examination of reason, or had been rejected by her.
>
> From the gate of reason there was a way to the throne of hope, by a craggy, slippery, and winding path, called the *streight of difficulty*, which those who entered with the permission of the guard endeavoured to climb.[5]

The "favourites of fancy" are shown in *Rambler* No. 67 to be seduced by ease. When they realize the difficulty of rational control, they turn "to the vale of idleness, from whence they [can] always have hope in prospect." By combating the human tendency to fix on easy absolutes, Reason must regulate and govern Imagination without overthrowing it, just as by analogy repentance and godliness imply not a denial of the sense of creatureliness but a regulation of it; a sense of inadequacy put to active use.

For Johnson true rationality and Christian faith are identical. He saw in religion the supreme exercise of both human faculties, or rather the ultimate subjection of Imagination to Reason. A full discussion of Johnson's particular religious beliefs is outside the scope of this book (although one might remark in passing that those critics who find nothing heterodox either in his faith or in his practice seem to have the stronger argument in the controversy about

[5] *Ibid.*, p. 320.

the kind of doctrine he adhered to).[6] What needs to be stressed here is the fact that there is no trace of either fideism or mysticism in his religious writings. Religious truth is the fruit of rational "reflection." Man knows, "when he *reflects calmly*, that the world is neither eternal, nor independent; that we neither were produced, nor are preserved by chance. But that heaven and earth, and the whole system of things, were created by an infinite and perfect Being, who still continues to superintend and govern them." [7] The great attraction of Christianity lies in the fact that it discourages imaginative speculations concerning the moral structure of the universe. Instead, it concentrates on the practical question of individual salvation. It discourages ease and looseness in favor of rational exercise. The virtues extolled by religion are all expressions of fulfilled Reason: "That men of *different opinions* should live at peace is the true effect of that *humility*, which *makes each esteem others better than himself*, and of that moderation which *reason approves*." [8]

The main value of religion is thus as a check upon Imagination's tendency to idealize the self. Man's proud subjective pursuit of earthly goals is transformed by religion into "usefulness" and virtue, since it calls attention to the common forms of belief which reflect the general condition of man. Rationality and godliness are one and the same:

The power of godliness is contained in the love of God and of our neighbor; in that sum of religion, in which, as we are told by the Saviour of the world, the law and the prophets are comprised. The love of God will engage us to trust in his protection, to acquiesce in his dispensations, to keep his laws, to meditate on his perfection, and to declare our confidence and submission, by profound and frequent adoration; to impress his glory on our minds by songs of praise, to inflame our gratitude by acts of thanksgiving, to strengthen our faith, and exalt our hope, by pious meditations; and to implore his protection of our imbecility, and his assistance of our frailty, by humble supplication; and when we love God with the whole heart, the power of godliness will be shown by steadiness in temptation, by patience in affliction, by faith in the Divine promises, by

---

[6] See, e.g., Donald Greene's "Theology and the Literary Scholar: A Review Article," *Canadian Journal of Theology*, XI (1965), 207–16—an attack on certain points made by Maurice J. Quinlan in *Samuel Johnson, A Layman's Religion*. See also my essay "Reason and Unreason in Johnson's Religion," *Modern Language Review*, LIV (1964), pp. 519–26.

[7] *Sermon XVI*. Quoted in Quinlan, pp. 44–45.

[8] *Sermon XI*. Quinlan, p. 150.

perpetual dread of sin, by continual aspirations after higher degrees of holiness, and contempt of the pains and pleasures of the world, when they obstruct the progress of religious excellence.[9]

Much has been written about Johnson's indebtedness to William Law, who was the principal early influence on his religious thought.[10] But what can hardly be overemphasized is the rational element in what Johnson found so appealing. If he was "overmatched" by Law, as he said, this was not at all due to some mystical or "enthusiastic" call to religion. What appealed to him in the *Serious Call to a Devout and Holy Life* was the instruction it offered in positive piety, Law's proclaimed intention to teach "the right use of the world"[11] and not at all to cast a shadow on the power of reason to reach religious conclusions. What overmatched Johnson in the *Serious Call* were argumentations such as:

> If a man had five fix'd years to live he could not possibly think at all, without intending to make the best of them *all*. When he saw his stay so short in this world, he must needs think that this was not a world for him; and when he saw how near he was to another world, that was eternal, he must surely think it necessary to be very dilligent in preparing himself for it.
>
> Now as reasonable as piety appears in such a circumstance of life, it is yet more reasonable in every circumstance of life, to every thinking man.
>
> For who but a madman can reckon that he has *five* years *certain* to come?
>
> And if it be reasonable and necessary to deny our worldly tempers, and live wholly unto God, because we are *certain* that we are to die at the end of five years; surely it must be much more reasonable and necessary, for us to live in the same spirit, because we have no *certainty*, that we shall *live five weeks*.[12]

Law was hardly appealing to unbelievers. He took faith for granted, and he argued for a life according to that faith and for positive piety as a rational course. "Now as reasonable as piety appears in such a circumstance of life, it is yet more reasonable in every circumstance"—the appeal is to the "thinking man," and it is the power of this appeal that made Johnson praise the *Serious Call* as "the finest piece of hortatory theology in any language."[13]

[9] *Sermon* XIII. Quinlan, p. 142.

[10] See Katherine C. Balderston, "Doctor Johnson and William Law," *PMLA* (1960), 382–94; Balderston, "Dr. Johnson's Use of William Law in the Dictionary," *Philological Quarterly* (1960), 379–88; Maurice J. Quinlan, *Samuel Johnson, A Layman's Religion*, pp. 3–26.

[11] William Law, *A Serious Call to a Devout and Holy Life, Adopted to the State and Condition of all Orders of Christians* (2nd ed.; London, 1732), chap. xiii, 209.

[12] *Ibid.*, 224–25.

[13] *Life*, II, 122.

Finally, the role of Reason in Johnson's religion becomes most apparent when we consider the fact that his thought, like Christianity itself, centers in the contemplation of mortality. Both human Imagination and human Reason become comprehensible only in terms of the central fact of death. And Johnson's own "fear of death," which has been the subject of much controversy,[14] was for him the final test of rationality. The lack of such rational fear appeared to him the most crucial of imaginative delusions. A great part of his insistence on the rationality of fearing death is based on the uncertainty of salvation; on the belief that "confidence with respect to futurity" has no part in "the character of a brave, a wise, or a good man," because "bravery has no place where it can avail nothing."[15] "Some people," he would say, "are not afraid, because they look upon salvation as the effect of an absolute decree, and think they feel in themselves the marks of sanctification. Others, and those *the most rational* in my opinion, look upon salvation as conditional; and as they never can be sure that they have complied with the conditions, they are afraid."[16] The sight of a man dying can and should cause "a confusion of passions, an awful stillness of sorrow, a gloomy terror without a name," and nothing is more irreligious *or irrational* than to react differently to death. The difference between cant about morality and the true sense of death becomes part of his general theory about the deceiving function of Imagination and the contrast between life as it is and as the needs of our mind make it appear.

The fear of death represents contact with one's true reality, a rational recognition of things as they are, and a conquest over Imagination, which, in this phase of Johnson's thought, represents the self-generating inventive power that enables us to live from moment to moment as if we were never to die. Johnson faces here that basic paradox of existence in time, the contradiction between the serenity or passion of our day to day pursuits and our rational ability to put those pursuits in their temporal perspective and value them accordingly: it is a knowledge possessed by everyone, yet life goes on as if it were not. Living in terms of the "Choice of Life"

[14] The best account is by J. H. Hagstrum, "On Doctor Johnson's Fear of Death," *ELH*, XIV (1947), 308–19.
[15] Letter to Mrs. Thrale, 10 March 1784, *Letters, II*, 138.
[16] *Life*, IV, 278.

(i.e., as if we were immortal) thus appears as the most widespread of "fallacies," the most prevalent of imaginative deceptions. Boswell once told Johnson that he had seen the execution of several convicts at Tyburn and that "none of them seemed under any concern."

JOHNSON: "Most of them, Sir, have never thought of it at all."
BOSWELL: "But is not the fear of death natural to man?"
JOHNSON: "*So much so, Sir, that the whole of life is but keeping away the thoughts of it.*"[17]

The full experience of mortality becomes something that can be achieved only by breaking the chain of imaginative habits and fully exercising the reason. "The general forgetfulness of the fragility of life" is a "fallacy" that is "so deeply rooted in the heart, and so *strongly guarded by hope and fear against the approach of reason,* that neither science nor experience can shake it, and we act as if life were without end, though we see and confess its uncertainty and shortness."[18] Our mortality is "one of those subjects, which, though of the utmost importance, and of indubitable certainty, are generally secluded from our regard, by the jollity of health, the hurry of employment, and even the calmer diversions of study and speculation; or if they become accidental topics of conversation and argument, yet rarely sink deep into the heart, but give occasion to some subtilties of reasoning, or elegancies of declamation, which are heard, applauded and forgotten."[19]

The inability to experience mortality as it should be experienced, in a full apprehension of the true state of affairs as Reason discloses it to be, becomes for Johnson the mark of Imagination's victory; this is how cant is identifiable on the one hand with irreligion and on the other with life as the very process of living in time makes it appear to itself. "The well-known and well-attested position, that life is short . . . may be heard among mankind by an attentive auditor, many times a day."[20] Many "sententious philosophers . . . repeat these aphorisms, merely because they have somewhere heard them . . . but no ideas are annexed to the words." The souls of such people "are mere pipes or organs, which transmit sounds, but do not understand them."[21] The urgency that informs all of Johnson's

[17] *Ibid.*, II, 93.
[18] *Rambler* No. 71, *Works*, II, 337.
[19] *Rambler* No. 54, *Works*, II, 259.
[20] *Rambler* No. 71, *Works*, II, 335.
[21] *Ibid.*, p. 334.

observations on Reason and Imagination is the product of an attempt to understand, by stripping experience of all its imaginative trappings, "the well-attested position, that life is short." Johnson's entire exposé of man's delusions and fallacies—in philosophy, in morals, in art, in day-to-day life—is reducible to his basic definition of man as a creature who seeks out many subtle ways of forgetting the unpleasant fact that he is destined to die.

ABBREVIATIONS IN NOTES

Works	*Dr. Johnson's Works*, ed. W. Pickering (11 vols.; London, 1825).
Letters	*The Letters of Samuel Johnson*, ed. R. W. Chapman (3 vols.; Oxford, 1952).
Diaries	*Samuel Johnson's Diaries, Prayers and Annals*, ed. E. L. McAdam with D. and M. Hyde (New Haven, Conn., 1958).
Lives	*Lives of the English Poets* (2 vols.; World's Classics; London, 1961).
Rasselas	*History of Rasselas Prince of Abyssinia*, ed. G. B. Hill (Oxford, 1887).
Life	*Boswell's Life of Johnson*, ed. G. B. Hill, rev. L. F. Powell (6 vols.; Oxford, 1934).
Thraliana	*Thraliana, The Diary of Mrs. Hester Lynch Thrale*, ed. K. C. Balderston (2 vols.; Oxford, 1951).
J.M.	*Johnsonian Miscellanies*, ed. G. B. Hill (2 vols.; Oxford, 1897).
On Shakespeare	*Johnson on Shakespeare*, ed. W. Raleigh (Oxford, 1952).

INDEX

designer:	Gerard Valerio
typesetter:	Baltimore Type and Composition Corporation
typefaces:	Garamond
printer:	Universal Lithographers, Inc.
paper:	P & S Olde Forge
binder:	Moore and Company, Inc.
cover material:	Columbia Riverside RV-1695